BREAK FREE

E'YEN A. GARDNER

Printed Word Publishing

BREAK FREE
Copyright © 2009 by E'yen A. Gardner

Printed Word Publishing
PO BOX 360812
Columbus, Ohio 43236

PH: 614-678-5353
FAX: 888-221-3166

www.pwpublish.com
pwpublish@yahoo.com

Printed in the United States of America

All Scripture bible references are from the King James Version of the Holy Bible.

All rights reserved. No part of this book may be reproduced or transmitted in any form or by any means without written permission of the author.

Book Editing: Maia R. Gardner, Senior Editor

Cover Design: Katawi K. Cato, Graphic Designer
 www.kcatodesign.com
 katawicato@gmail.com

ISBN: 978-0-615-29402-5
Library of Congress Control Number: 2009910461

Acknowledgements

Jesus I am set free by your amazing love. Thank you for sharing your amazing truths with me. I am humbled by your grace and covered by your mercy. Thank you for looking past my imperfections. I know that this book will set your people free.

Maia you are my best friend, my love, my pastor and my crown. I am so thankful that you are in my life. You provoke me to go after all that God has for me. You are an amazing gift that I cherish everyday. You have a great passion for God and I am inspired by your relationship with Him. I love you Maia.

Arin, J'sun, Raya, Lesa, Kyan, and Bria you guys inspire me to seek God with everything I have. You are my inspiration. My desire is that you will walk in the liberty of Christ and allow Him break down any walls that confront you. You are so special and you are anointed to walk in the land God has promised you.

Thank you Katawi for another great book cover design. I truly appreciate your work.

Contents

Preface 7
Introduction 11
Called Out of Ignorance 15
Untested Armor 23
Drilling for Gold 31
One Stone 43
The Real Party 53
Pressed Through Giants 59

~ Part 2: Receiving our Reward ~

Abiding in Christ 69
Living in the Grace of God 85
Running the Race 99
Birthing a Son 113
Sown Seeds of Promise 119
What is our Reward? 127

≈ Preface ≈

What has us bound? What is it that we need to *Break Free* from? It is amazing how many things hold us captive throughout our entire lives. Maybe it was the scorn of our peers, or the abuse of an unloving parent. Each one of us comes from a vast demographic of backgrounds, involving situations that lead to our various strongholds. Regardless, we all receive the same call.

The call is to *Break Free*! *Break Free* from our past, our fears, and our limitations, and walk into the land that has been prepared for us to reign in! We have been faithful with what God has given us, and now it is time for us to cross over our "Jordan River" and possess the land that has been ordained for us.

In this land there are many obstacles that we will have to deal with, and everything we have learned in the "wilderness" is *essential* for us to overcome the

Preface

giants and fears that lie ahead of us. The giants are *real* and the walls are fortified.

Nevertheless, we have seen miraculous things done for us in the "wilderness" and God has provided for every one of our needs. He has armed us with power through our experiences and our relationship with Him, and now we must journey over, equipped with only the knowledge that was given to us in the "wilderness."

This is the place where our lives are squeezed and our faith is attacked by the inhabitants of the land who are unwilling to give up without a fight. Will we be willing to face our fears? Perhaps the *real* question is: will we rule in the land of abundance or will the *giants*?

We have dreamed of this day for so long, but as we approach the fertile grounds of our destiny, we are faced with the choice to either stay in our current comfort zone of the "wilderness," or cross over to face new challenges that will push us further into understanding the treasure that dwells inside of us. Fear not and be of good courage. All that we see ahead has been predestined for us to overcome and rule over!

This book will confront many of the obstacles and pitfalls that every believer has to face when crossing

Preface

over into their "promised land." If we are willing to be honest with ourselves, we will learn how to conquer our fears and embrace the challenges that have been laid out before us, for the Glory of God. Commit yourself to journeying with me to our ordained place in the plan of God!

~ Introduction ~

Standing at the crest of change, the decision to cross over into the land that is promised to us and all that follow, is scary. No longer can we hide behind the shadows of others, for we understand that we have been chosen to lead God's children into a life of peace and abundance. As thoughts race through our minds, we cannot ignore the magnitude of the decision we must make: Will we *fight* for peace?

The current inhabitant's time has expired. It is now time for their eviction, and time for the occupancy of the people of God. As we regard the frailty of His people, we are reminded of God's Word, and it rings clearly in our heart: "Have not I commanded thee? Be strong and of a good courage; be not afraid, neither be thou dismayed: for the LORD thy God is with thee whithersoever thou goest," (Joshua 1:9).

True fear encompasses us as we realize that crossing this "river" will be the end of the reproach of

Introduction

our past. "And the LORD said unto Joshua, This day have I rolled away the reproach of Egypt from off you," (Joshua 5:9).

Don't fear. Be strong and have "good courage." What does God mean by these words? What does He see that He is not telling *us*? In spite of some apprehension, we are empowered by the assurance that God is with us. Our decision in this moment to cross over is what we were made for. The sandals that we have worn are of no use on the other side of this river for every step we take now is on holy ground – separated for God's use (Joshua 1:3).

The baggage that we have carried throughout our journey to the edge of change must now remain behind, for it can not help us on the other side. We must say goodbye to our comforts, successes, failures, routines, titles, conveniences, and tears, while girding ourselves with the hope that what we have learned will propel us into fulfilling our destiny.

Break Free is more than a saying, it is our *calling*. God has prepared an abundant measure for His people, but if we refuse to continue and lead those that follow us into the land of promise, we shackle the blessings that lay await for our consummation. Many are waiting for the opportunity to experience the "promised land." They can see it, but it is *our* calling to

Break Free

lead them into it. Will we break free from our methods, our religious traditions and our commandments, to obey the voice of God and cross over into our ordained place of rest?

In order to lead a people, we must confront ourselves on this journey and not fear the things that need to be released from within us. Only those individuals that tap into the strength of God are going to be able to handle the road ahead; it will take every ounce of courage to deal with the internal battle of ourselves and the external barrier that the giants of the land present.

As we take our first steps towards change, we must realize that we will never travel back to Egypt nor the "wilderness," but will only go forward by the Word that God has placed in our hearts. "And he gave Joshua the son of Nun a charge, and said, Be strong and of a good courage: for thou shalt bring the children of Israel into the land which I sware unto them: and I will be with thee," (Deuteronomy 31:23).

≈ Called out of Ignorance ≈

"For they being ignorant of God's righteousness, and going about to establish their own righteousness, have not submitted themselves unto the righteousness of God," (Romans 10:3).

We are all in pursuit of the same thing. We live out our entire lives trying to make our dreams become a reality and we tell our loved ones that we cannot wait until God blesses us to live in the manifestation of our dreams. We want to see our children grow up and reach their dreams. We encourage our friends to hold onto their dreams and to never give up. Our dreams are individually different, but at the same time, still uniformly resemble one another.

However, we all must face some unavoidable questions. Is my dream in God's Will and purpose for my life? Am I being driven by God, or is it just *me*? What will I do when my dream becomes a reality? What will I pursue when I remain void of fulfillment?

Called out of Ignorance

Many of us come just short of seeing our dreams become a reality because of our ignorance. We are ignorant to *what* the dream is, *whose* dream it is, and the *purpose* of the dream. Most importantly, we are ignorant to God's working power in manifesting the dream in our lives.

~ Dream or Nightmare? ~

Many of us are living lives that are unfulfilled. We have families, careers, and ministries, but there is something still missing. There is no evidence of the presence of God working in our lives, and His power remains void as we routinely manage our responsibilities. We have painfully seen loved ones suffer from diseases that they do not recover from. We fervently pray for changes in our communities, but they continue to worsen. We cry out to God for Him to deliver us from our financial troubles, but we remain in poverty. Why, in the pursuit of reaching for our dreams, is our reality a "nightmare?"

We try to avoid facing our "nightmares" because it is easier to ignore our fears and insecurities, rather than face them. Have you ever wondered what the ending of your "nightmare" will be? We wake up when the ending seems hopeless. We accept the wonderful dreams of mansions, cars, and tranquility, but we deny what relevance a nightmare of despair, violence, and death may have in our lives.

Are all "nightmares" evil and unholy, or do we just lack understanding of what the Spirit of God is trying to reveal to us? Is our ignorance *truly* bliss? God desires to bless us, not through ignorance, but through wisdom and understanding. "My son, attend unto my wisdom, and bow thine ear to my understanding," (Proverbs 5:1). We are fearful of our "nightmares" because we don't understand the relevance of them in our lives. When God begins to unlock the doors of understanding, we become empowered to overcome our fears. We cannot ignore our fears anymore – we cannot avoid them at *any* cost. Our fears are hindering us from obtaining the promises and provision that God has prepared for us. So, we *must* overcome our fears through faith.

~ *Bubble of Ignorance* ~

Our false sense of security has placed us inside of a "bubble," where we believe that we have complete control of our lives. "Having the understanding darkened, being alienated from the life of God through the ignorance that is in them, because of the blindness of their heart:" (Ephesians 4:18). We avoid the agony of defeat and we ignore the reality of our captivity. We may have a *form* of God's light working through us, but

Called out of Ignorance

we are still being held captive by our fears. What we regard is not reality, because it is covered by our fears, and we live enslaved to what we are afraid of.

What has polluted our very being, causing us to live inside a "bubble?" Why have our lives been subject to our fears instead of being subject to God? The answer is: our *ignorance*. If we ignore something long enough, we will begin to believe only what we want to believe, rather than the truth, therefore, forming a "bubble." Many of us as Christians ignore the fleshly addictions and habits that control us and continue believing that God is pleased with our lives. Few of us even come to grips with the reality that our actions are keeping us from God's presence. Nevertheless, if we ignore the "bad" in us, does that mean that it is gone? On the contrary, for *ignoring* our issues only puts more distance between us and God.

Have you ever noticed that the more you ignore something, the "bigger" it becomes? Our "bubbles" of ignorance have reached their capacity and God is about to "burst" them. If you have ever popped a bubble, you understand that whatever is inside the bubble becomes completely saturated by the substance that created the bubble.

As God bursts our "bubbles," the things that we have been ignoring for years are now ever present on us and we cannot ignore them any longer. What will we do? What *can* we do when the things we have been trying to ignore are now "covering" us? Our ignorance has clouded our visions, shattered our dreams and filled our lives with wounds and scars that have never been healed. When our "bubble" is "burst," we can no longer ignore God, but now turn *towards* Him.

I will never forget the torment I lived in when I tried to ignore the secrets and lies that I hid from my wife. Have you ever held something from someone that you love? The longer I held the truth from her, the more the lie tormented me each day. I justified myself, claiming that since I lied *before* I was "saved," God had forgiven me of my sins. Yet, every time the thought surfaced, I still felt convicted and shameful. The more I grew in God and in my relationship with my wife, the more I fought to tell her the truth.

Years went by, and I wanted to confess to her, but it was just easier to ignore the thoughts and act like it never happened. By justifying myself though, I was ignorantly giving place for the enemy to keep me from being free in my marriage. The enemy flooded my thoughts, telling me that if I was honest with her, she would leave me. However, if we don't confront the *seed* of lies, it gives place for them to take root in us and we become bound to the "prison cell" that those lies create.

Called out of Ignorance

I ran from the truth everyday, and because of the guilt that I felt, my marriage *and* my relationship with God were strained. Finally, one day I was convinced that I had to come clean with my wife, whether she decided to leave me or not. I could not live with the lie, the guilt, or the frustration any longer. I hurt my wife by lying and as a result of coming clean, I became saturated in the truth that I had been ignoring. It was a painful process, but it was necessary for us to move forward and live a life in a marriage with no lies or secrets.

God wants us to be free from the lies, the secrets and the strongholds that we have in our closets. Will we open the door to our secret closet? Will we allow God to come in and evict everything that has been holding us down from living free in Him? His voice *cannot* go unheard, for our ears have been unclogged of our fears. "Out of heaven he made thee to hear his voice, that he might instruct thee: and upon earth he shewed thee his great fire; and thou heardest his words out of the midst of the fire," (Deuteronomy 4:36). What will we do when we hear our Creator calling us out of our ignorance? God is knocking on our door and He is ready for our response.

We must understand that the liberation of our minds is essential to living outside of the "bubble" of ignorance. So, when God speaks and makes us aware of our issues, we must be thankful that He is empowering us to be changed. Through the Spirit, we become new, for it is through His consuming fire that the "giant" of ignorance is destroyed. The Word of God – *the sword* – cuts off the "head" of the "giant" of ignorance and we no longer are held captive, but rather become liberated to live in the awareness and power of God's presence in our lives.

≈ Untested Armor ≈

"And he stood and cried unto the armies of Israel, and said unto them, Why are ye come out to set your battle in array? am not I a Philistine, and ye servants to Saul? choose you a man for you, and let him come down to me. If he be able to fight with me, and to kill me, then will we be your servants: but if I prevail against him, and kill him, then shall ye be our servants, and serve us. And the Philistine said, I defy the armies of Israel this day; give me a man, that we may fight together," (I Samuel 17:8-10).

Goliath, the giant of Gath, appeared before the fearful armies of Israel for forty days. As a result of their fear, Israel ignored the call of the giant to go to battle. Not *one* considered fighting Goliath, for their fear of this massive man clouded their vision of a victorious outcome. "For Israel and the Philistines had put the battle in array, army against army," (I Samuel 17:21). Yes, the armies of Israel were armed for the battle, but they were unable to fight, being paralyzed by their fear. "And all the men of Israel, when they saw

Untested Armor

the man, fled from him, and were sore afraid," (I Samuel 17:24).

What was the use of being armed, if they were not willing to fight? Goliath had no respect for Israel or their king, but no one was even willing to confront him about his arrogance. So, day after day the armies of Israel armed themselves, but as they heard Goliath, they allowed his words to control their actions.

Like Israel, many of *us* are equipped with the armor of God. The bible tells us, in Ephesians 6:13-17, that we have our Sword (the Word of God), we have our Shield (our Faith), we have our Breastplate (God's Righteousness), and we have our Helmet (our Salvation). Nevertheless, none of this armor is of any use if we are too afraid to even face our "giants." How many times have we allowed someone's words to dictate what *we* do? We can get excited and empowered by what God reveals to us, but then be so easily influenced by the discouraging words of an unbeliever (someone who doubts what God has shown us). We don't realize that when we ignore the calling of the "giant," we are really ignoring the call of God and the work that He wants to do through us. So, we remain weak and paralyzed because we regard the words of our enemy *higher* than we regard the words of God.

Break Free

It is our *destiny* to slay "giants," but we also have to recognize that it is our enemy's job to keep us out of the fight. "Lest Satan should get an advantage of us: for we are not ignorant of his devices," (2 Corinthians 2:11). If he can get us to ignore our "giants" and keep us paralyzed in our armor, we will never realize that we have been separated from the presence *and* the power of God. God's presence is in the midst of the battle for those that depend on His strength in battle. Yes, God has equipped us for battle, and we brag and boast of our victory, but only up until we are actually *standing* before a "giant."

Our churches are full of "armed" saints that are stuck in their "tents" of comfort. When the opportunity arises to fight the "giants" for the lost souls in our community, we turn away and cleave to our safety net – our *church*. The weapon of evangelism is ignored and replaced with the feeling of comfort in only praising God under our "tent." Therefore, no one is able to see the power of God, for we have covered *His* Spirit with the spirit of *fear*. We are trying to fight spiritual battles while in our comfort zones in the church, and God stands alone waiting for us to come out and be a vessel of His. We claim to be glorifying and magnifying the name of Jesus, but until we are properly positioned, our actions continue to minimize the power of our God right in front of our enemies.

Untested Armor

Every time we ignore the call to fight, we allow our "giants" to continue on disrespecting our God. We present ourselves powerless through avoiding the opportunity to demonstrate dominion over the enemies of God. No matter how we try to mask our fears with fine clothes, titles, swelling words and a persuasive voice, it is all for naught if we are not in our rightful position in the battle. The enemy can not take our authority or our new birthright to fight; all he can do is discourage us from even trying. What will we do? Will we continue to disobey the voice of the living God or will we surrender our fears and doubts to Him so that we can be placed in the line of fire?

~ *The Covered Body* ~

"But it came to pass, when Nebuchadrezzar king of Babylon came up into the land, that we said, Come, and let us go to Jerusalem for fear of the army of the Chaldeans, and for fear of the army of the Syrians: so we dwell at Jerusalem. Then came the word of the LORD unto Jeremiah, saying, Thus saith the LORD of hosts, the God of Israel; Go and tell the men of Judah and the inhabitants of Jerusalem, Will ye not receive instruction to hearken to my words? saith the LORD," (Jeremiah 35:11-13).

Either our prayers are not being heard, or we are *ignoring* the answers that God has spoken over our lives. Our inner being is fearful of the fight in front of us because we have missed the instructions of God. The more we are provoked to fight, the more fearful we become of the outcome. We would rather ignore each and every spiritual giant rather than allowing our lives to be vulnerable to death. However, are you really *living* if your life is consumed with fear?

Our churches have become the household of *fear*, not *faith*. The conditions of our churches are based on the *feeling* of the anointing and not the genuine presence of God. Where is the evidence of our relationship with God? The truth is, we have separated our lives from our *relationship* with God. We "put on" religion when we are in church, but outside of church our "real" lives are consumed with carnal habits that provoke us to dwell in fear (Romans 8:6). We are exhorted to simply adorn ourselves with "holy garments," but our unseen lives are consumed in sin. "Howbeit in vain do they worship me, teaching for doctrines the commandments of men," (Mark 7:7). We have left the will of God and replaced it with the will of Man. "And [Jesus] said unto them, full well ye reject the commandment of God, that ye may keep your own tradition," (Mark 7:9).

As we cleave to our spiritual leaders, we don't realize that they are just as afraid of the giant as we are. "When Saul and all Israel heard those words of the Philistine, they were dismayed, and greatly afraid," (I

Untested Armor

Samuel 17:11). Yes, our spiritual leaders have inspired us to arm ourselves for battle, but in closed quarters, they too stand paralyzed in fear. Everyone has found inspiration through them, but they have lost sight of the presence of God because a giant has come in between them and their destiny. So, they turn from their destiny and preach from their tents of stagnation, questioning, why risk losing everything by fighting the giant when we can keep what we have obtained by just *ignoring* the "giant?" However, is it our divine destiny to arm the people of God but never demonstrate the power of our weapons in battle? "And from the days of John the Baptist until now the kingdom of heaven suffereth violence, and the violent take it by force," (Matthew 11:12).

We have enlarged our churches to resemble a kingdom, but truthfully, we are only worshiping God under a "tent." Some of our churches have become so prosperous because they remain unseen to the world. This prosperity does not bother the enemy, because he does not care about how much we worship or praise God, as long as it is hidden. Sadly, we will not openly praise God among unbelievers. It makes them *and* us very uncomfortable, because we are ignoring the urge to proclaim liberty to the lost souls of the world.

What has covered the body of Christ from the world? Why has the power of the name of Jesus been forgotten? We have been given a name that is above every name, but we are ignorant of its power. We have forgotten that the name of Jesus carries a purging fire with it! We use the name so loosely that we can not recognize the purging that incorporates the proclamation of Jesus.

When God convicts us, we can either remain in our current state, or we can allow Him to transform us by His Word. Truth is our weapon against ignorance, for it destroys the walls that separate us from God's words. "And ye shall know the truth, and the truth shall make you free," (John 8:32). Our ignorance can shackle us, and it is our decision whether we will stay in bondage, or be set free. The truth is what cleanses us, and prepares us for our walk with God. We need to hear the truth and *Break Free*! Even though God's truth leads us out of our ignorance, giants still stand in the way of our destiny. Nevertheless, now is the time to face those giants, face our fears, and unleash what is in us to slay them where they stand. It is time for battle!

≈Drilling for Gold≈

All of us are guilty of ignoring our fears and being paralyzed in our "bubbles" of comfort at some point in time, but there is a David-like spirit in us that yearns to be unleashed against the giants that have kept us captive to our fears. Nothing was more important to David than his relationship with God, and as a result, any person or thing that came against God's authority became an enemy of his as well (James 4:4).

Unfortunately, we do not recognize the "David" in us, because we have befriended the things that are the enemies of God. We do not want to destroy them because they have given us so much pleasure and enjoyment. The "friends" we are holding on to may not be "sinful," but we must recognize that *anything* we hold in high regard has the potential to become an enemy of God. The time and attention that we give those things has the potential to draw us away from not only His voice, but also His presence.

Drilling for Gold

What is unique and special about the like-spirit of David inside of us is that it is absolutely *fearless*. It does not regard surrounding circumstances; it only regards the power of God. David was not reliant on his *own* strength, but on the presence of God to demonstrate *His* power in the midst of overwhelming odds. Therefore we can also be sure that no situation is hopeless. When we allow the "David" in *us* to be unleashed, it allows the Spirit of God to take over and work on our behalf.

David represents the side of us that is not obligated to the many rules and regulations of men, but rather one who is seen as radical and different. In other words, we do not regard the laws of men *higher* than the voice of God. Many do not understand the reasoning of our David-like persona because it is not influenced by "common sense." It is influenced by *faith*. We believe in things that, naturally, make no sense and are impossible, which causes us to remain firm in our stance when standing on the promises of God.

The "David" in us openly proclaims the goodness and power of God with no regards of who hears or what other people may think. Our focus is not to be purposely different or controversial, but to simply speak and act upon the Word that God has revealed to us. "For we cannot but speak the things which we have

Break Free

seen and heard," (Acts 4:20). As was David, the "David" in us is untamed to society, yet totally surrendered to God.

~ *Stuck in Position* ~

"And some of the Hebrews went over Jordan to the land of Gad and Gilead. As for Saul, he was yet in Gilgal, and all the people followed him trembling. And he tarried seven days, according to the set time that Samuel had appointed: but Samuel came not to Gilgal; and the people were scattered from him. And Saul said, Bring hither a burnt offering to me, and peace offerings. And he offered the burnt offering. And it came to pass, that as soon as he had made an end of offering the burnt offering, behold, Samuel came; and Saul went out to meet him, that he might salute him. And Samuel said, What hast thou done? And Saul said, Because I saw that the people were scattered from me, and that thou camest not within the days appointed, and that the Philistines gathered themselves together at Michmash; Therefore said I, The Philistines will come down now upon me to Gilgal, and I have not made supplication unto the LORD: I forced myself therefore, and offered a burnt offering. And Samuel said to Saul, Thou hast done foolishly: thou hast not kept the commandment of the LORD thy God, which he commanded thee: for now would the LORD have established thy kingdom upon Israel for ever. But now thy kingdom shall not continue: the LORD hath sought him a man after his own heart, and the LORD hath commanded him to be captain over his people, because thou hast not kept that which the LORD commanded thee," (I Samuel 13:7-14).

Drilling for Gold

King Saul was given a word from God by the prophet Samuel, who instructed Saul to wait seven days until he came, so a sacrifice could be offered before the Lord. Saul waited as he was instructed, but became very anxious on the seventh day because the people were becoming very impatient. Since Saul decided to regard the people instead of patiently waiting on Samuel, he ultimately disobeyed the word of God and sacrificed the animals himself. He rebelled against the word of God because he could not handle the pressure of disappointing the people. Yes, Saul *was* the anointed king, but he took his sight off of God and severed the kingdom from his rule.

It is a joy when we can compare ourselves to the heroes in the bible such as David, but in reality, many of us tend to act more like King Saul. Like Saul, we regard what the people surrounding us think, *higher* than we regard the words and instructions of God. We continually fall short of God's glory in efforts to please Him and men because it simply does not work (Galatians 1:10). If we think about it, there would have been no need for *David*, if Saul would have been obedient to God's instructions. Unfortunately, just like King Saul, we bury ourselves in the cares of this world and the word of God is choked from our lives.

The "King Saul" in us is well-liked and well spoken of, because we appear to fulfill the requirements of a great leader for we exude good character and morals. We start off with the right intentions, but as we receive the applause of others, we become unconcerned with the approval of God.

Many times, we are in our rightful positions, but we fail to surrender ourselves to God's authority and try to handle our obligations in our *own* strength. Why aren't we desperate enough to stay in close fellowship with God? Why are we willing to lose the presence of God for the approval of men? It is one thing to be *anointed*, but it is another to live in *submission* to His anointing.

Like David, Saul was not afraid of his enemies. It was not until God's Spirit left Saul, that he became afraid, because he knew he had to fight them on his own. "But the Spirit of the LORD departed from Saul, and an evil spirit from the LORD troubled him," (I Samuel 16:14). The "Saul" in us causes us to remain content and unaffected by the choices we make until we are confronted by an enemy that will have no mercy on us. We continue in our bad habits until we are placed into a situation where we see no way out. It is not until *then*, that we are sorry for what we have done and want God to surround us and take control. Saul's choices led him to hide from his enemies for forty days, along with the understanding that God was no longer with him. In

Drilling for Gold

those forty days, Saul had many opportunities to repent and turn to God, but instead he stayed stuck in his "pit."

There was another king in the bible, King Ahab, who did not follow in the footsteps of Saul, but took advantage of God's mercy:

> "But there was none like unto Ahab, which did sell himself to work wickedness in the sight of the LORD, whom Jezebel his wife stirred up. And he did very abominably in following idols, according to all things as did the Amorites, whom the LORD cast out before the children of Israel. And it came to pass, when Ahab heard those words, that he rent his clothes, and put sackcloth upon his flesh, and fasted, and lay in sackcloth, and went softly. And the word of the LORD came to Elijah the Tishbite, saying, Seest thou how Ahab humbleth himself before me? because he humbleth himself before me, I will not bring the evil in his days: but in his son's days will I bring the evil upon his house," (I Kings 21:25-29).

Ahab was an evil king in the sight of God. He did horrible things and provoked the children of Israel to worship other gods. After allowing a man to be murdered in pursuit of more land, the word of God came in judgment against him. King Ahab rent his clothes and fasted, and God ultimately showed him mercy. Saul, though, was too proud to turn to God. He could have lived a prosperous and victorious life, but instead, the words of Goliath influenced him to live in fear; allowing David the opportunity to go boldly before the giant.

~ *Stuck in Sand* ~

So many times, *we* have lost our way in *our* walk with God. We, too, have been influenced by the "wrong" things *or* the "wrong" people, and have become captivated by the cares of this world. In addition, when God speaks to us about our wicked ways, we just dismiss His words and continue on in our "mess." Some of us try to get out of our "mess," our *own* way, but it acts like quicksand – the more we move, the deeper we sink. It is only through God's mercy, when we turn ourselves over to Him, that we are liberated from our methods *and* our "mess."

Sadly, we don't turn to God from our "mess" until we are on the verge of being consumed by it, and *then* we suddenly want Him to "make a way out of no way." When we choose to follow this self-sufficient route, we never learn the lesson *or* the benefit of staying close to our Father. Instead, when we are presented with opportunities to enjoy the pleasures of the world, we deliberately turn our backs to Him because we are certain that He will forgive us and deliver us from destruction.

Drilling for Gold

However, we can not *fully* appreciate our heavenly Father if we only call Him when our situations are too unbearable to handle on our own. Aren't you tired of being the child that only calls on your Father when the situation is dire? When will we put away our childish ways, and "grow up" into the person we were created to be? "When I was a child, I spake as a child, I understood as a child, I thought as a child: but when I became a man, I put away childish things," (I Corinthians 13:11).

Thank the Lord for His mercy to love us in spite of our childish mistakes and failures. If only we could tap into the greatness that is hidden deep within us, we could really know God and His plan for our lives.

~ *Drilling for Gold* ~

"Again, the kingdom of heaven is like unto treasure hid in a field; the which when a man hath found, he hideth, and for joy thereof goeth and selleth all that he hath, and buyeth that field," (Matthew 13:44).

When an oil company is searching and drilling for oil, the workers must dig at least two miles into the ground until they reach what they call, "liquid gold." In the process of drilling, they run into plenty of pitfalls, but their determination pushes them to continue digging. In spite of all the dirt that comes out and plasters on the workers, they are not willing to stop until they reach the

Break Free

"treasure" that they have set their confidence in reaching. They are unsure of whether the outcome will be as they envisioned, but the "treasure" is worth the risk of pursuit.

We too, must be completely invested in reaching the "liquid gold" that is within *us*. If we do not discover what is inside of us, we will be intimidated like King Saul. However, if we recognize the God whom we serve and His power in our lives, we will begin to depend on Him to manifest His promises. No, the work is not easy, and we will run into many obstacles along the way. Nevertheless, it is worth it all to be connected to the "treasures" that God planted in us before He even laid the foundations of the world, and we will be able to take dominion over the "land" that was promised to us.

We have to understand that everything we need is *inside* of us, for God created us with purpose and gifts – set apart and unique to the world – already in mind. We will undoubtedly stay slaves to our ignorance until we commit ourselves to the "drilling process" of God, and allow Him to draw out all the dirt and filthiness that is blocking us from our destiny. When God works to strike the core of our being, the hidden treasures are manifested in abundance, so the world can see the magnificent power of our God and give Him the glory (2 Corinthians 4:6-7).

Drilling for Gold

The "treasure" in us is reconnected to the One who sowed it; He then is able to exhibit His Power *and* Glory to all who come in contact with us. We desperately need to be aware that God has sown purpose in us and placed us into the earth. Even though our outward appearances or circumstances may not be appealing to us right now, when He is done with us, we will be a treasured commodity that will satisfy the *many* needs of His people.

The "drilling" process that we go through can not compare to *what* and *where* we are about to go. Oh how joy and thanksgiving has filled our hearts as we experience the riches of God's wisdom and knowledge through our newfound connection to our Father. It is amazing to see the manifestation of God's power in our lives.

The issue that we now run into is how to distribute the "treasure" from the source, to those that are in need. There has to be a vessel strong enough to carry God's treasure to its intended destination. When the commodity that we have in our possession stays put where we found it, it is ineffective and useless because it is not fulfilling its purpose. Wisdom is of no use if it is not imparted to those that are ignorant. Courage is of no use if it has not inspired the fearful to change. There is no point to having such special gifts if they remain hidden to the people that they are intended to serve.

Break Free

There is an undeniable urge that we have to maintain and manage the distribution of our treasure, but the results always lead to a dead end. God has connected us to His greatness, and *He* is the one that will distribute the measure of our gift to meet the needs of His people. We will remain stuck at the 'dead end' until we heed to the guidance of the Holy Spirit in our lives. It is our responsibility to carry the treasure, but it is God who steers us in the direction that we should go.

≈ One Stone ≈

In the presence of all of his family, David was anointed to be king of Israel. Despite his father witnessing him receive such a great honor, David was still regarded as someone less than ordinary, and for years remained as a shepherd over his father's sheep. Though God saw greatness in David, he was still regarded as the "least" in the sight of his family.

~ *Divine Isolation* ~

Have you ever been regarded as mediocre? Have you ever been told that you will never be successful or accomplish anything in life? God has anointed *us* for His use as well, but the world sees us – like they saw David – as "young and ruddy." Our greatness is ignored by people who refuse to believe that we are of any more value than what *they* have perceived. Many people do not know the battles that God has given us victory in, they have not witnessed the amazing worship experiences we have had in His presence, and they have not heard the songs that have be written in our hearts during the intimacy of our stillness. Nevertheless, it is all insignificant, for others just see us as out of touch with "reality," and only having a few "sheep."

Many of us have experienced rejection and have been given resentful looks because of our uniqueness and for the special qualities that we hold. However, they misinterpret our freedom for youthful exuberance, and their ignorance does not allow them to understand our divine place in their lives. They offensively say, "God speaks to me, so what makes *you* so special?" They so desperately try to discourage us and place us into the same bondage of conformity that has held *them* captive. In their hearts, they wonder why we are so happy, yet they desire to be the same.

It is so unfortunate that in the midst of our freedom, we are ignorant to the captivity of God's people. We have experienced victory upon victory in our isolation from the world, while the people of God have been stuck in a pit of defeat, with their fears keeping them enslaved. They question if we see the state of emergency that they are in, and why we act as if we have no care in the world. They do not understand, however, that it is in our *seclusion*, that we receive the much desired answers to the questions of life. In our

Break Free

understanding of who God is, we fear Him *only*, and no one or nothing matters more to us than pleasing Him.

~ *Moment of Destiny* ~

"And Jesse said unto David his son, Take now for thy brethren an ephah of this parched corn, and these ten loaves, and run to the camp of thy brethren; And carry these ten cheeses unto the captain of their thousand, and look how thy brethren fare, and take their pledge. Now Saul, and they, and all the men of Israel, were in the valley of Elah, fighting with the Philistines. And David rose up early in the morning, and left the sheep with a keeper, and took, and went, as Jesse had commanded him; and he came to the trench, as the host was going forth to the fight, and shouted for the battle. For Israel and the Philistines had put the battle in array, army against army. And David left his carriage in the hand of the keeper of the carriage, and ran into the army, and came and saluted his brethren. And as he talked with them, behold, there came up the champion, the Philistine of Gath, Goliath by name, out of the armies of the Philistines, and spake according to the same words: and David heard them," (I Samuel 17:17-23).

Through our obedience, we run right into our *destiny*. David was instructed by his father to take cheese "sandwiches" to his brothers that were fighting with the armies of Israel. When he went to fulfill his father's orders, he heard a man speaking, and what this man said *infuriated* him. David questioned, "How dare this man speak to God's people with such arrogance and conceit?" However, he was ignorant to the fact the man had been speaking in this manner for forty days! David did not regard Goliath as a giant but simply as a man, and could not believe that he had the audacity to come against the God of Israel. So, when David heard the words of Goliath, he was provoked to stand up to the enemy of God and become the vessel that God used to demonstrate His power to the world. David was not concerned with the fears of the people, like Saul, he was focused on the man that had no regard for his God.

> "And Eliab his eldest brother heard when he spake unto the men; and Eliab's anger was kindled against David, and he said, Why camest thou down hither? and with whom hast thou left those few sheep in the wilderness? I know thy pride, and the naughtiness of thine heart; for thou art come down that thou mightest see the battle... and Saul said to David, Thou art not able to go against this Philistine to fight with him: for thou art but a youth, and he a man of war from his youth," (I Samuel 17:28-33).

David faced opposition through Eliab, his older brother. Even King Saul doubted David's ability to defeat the giant of Gath, but their words did not sway David for his confidence was rooted in God. David, as he did with the lion and bear, he went to defend and fight for the *"sheep"* again, for *this* time, Israel was the *"sheep"* that belonged to God and no enemy was going to devour what was God's:

Break Free

"And David said unto Saul, Thy servant kept his father's sheep, and there came a lion, and a bear, and took a lamb out of the flock: And I went out after him, and smote him, and delivered it out of his mouth: and when he arose against me, I caught him by his beard, and smote him, and slew him. Thy servant slew both the lion and the bear: and this uncircumcised Philistine shall be as one of them, seeing he hath defied the armies of the living God. David said moreover, The LORD that delivered me out of the paw of the lion, and out of the paw of the bear, he will deliver me out of the hand of this Philistine. And Saul said unto David, Go, and the LORD be with thee," (I Samuel 17:34-37).

The "future" king of Israel could have easily ignored the words of Goliath and went back to where he was comfortable and tend to his sheep. No man would have looked down on that decision, for he was just a young man who was not trained to fight soldiers. *David*, though, could not walk away and allow the enemy to continue to mock the armies of the living God any longer. So, he went before the people of Israel, and the only way to reclaim the "sheep" was to slay the man that stood in his way.

~ Armor of Grace ~

"And Saul armed David with his armour, and he put an helmet of brass upon his head; also he armed him with a coat of mail. And David girded his sword upon his armour, and he assayed to go; for he had not proved

One Stone

it. And David said unto Saul, I cannot go with these; for I have not proved them. And David put them off him. And he took his staff in his hand, and chose him five smooth stones out of the brook, and put them in a shepherd's bag which he had, even in a scrip; and his sling was in his hand: and he drew near to the Philistine," (I Samuel 17:38-40).

For David, the armor of the king would not work, for David was not and had never been trained to be a solider. David was a *warrior*; he was not subject to the methods of a solider, he was only subject to the plan of God. So, David went to the brook and drew five stones out of the water (representing the armor of God). David had no way of defeating Goliath himself, but through the grace of God he was perfectly armed for his battle against the giant. Instead of relying on tradition, or his own thinking, David carried the Breastplate of Righteousness, the Gospel of Peace, the Shield of Faith, the Helmet of Salvation, and the Sword of the Spirit (Ephesians 6:14-17).

In every battle, *we* must also be armed with our "five stones" of Grace if we are to obtain victory in Christ Jesus. Our fears can keep us bound to the "law," causing us to only be armed with a natural armor. In which, we will not be armed with the *grace* of God to run to our giants with only our faith and destroy them where they stand.

Break Free

David drew near Goliath, and the giant did what everyone else had done to David – underestimated him:

> "And when the Philistine looked about, and saw David, he disdained him: for he was but a youth, and ruddy, and of a fair countenance. And the Philistine said unto David, Am I a dog, that thou comest to me with staves? And the Philistine cursed David by his gods," (I Samuel 17:42-43).

David was accustomed to this rejection and demeaning attitude, for he was hardly noticed by his own family, so it was not going to affect his performance in battle. If God had not conditioned and prepared David for the belittling from Goliath, those words would have thrown him off focus from what his purpose was; which was to destroy the works of his enemy:

> "Then said David to the Philistine, Thou comest to me with a sword, and with a spear, and with a shield: but I come to thee in the name of the LORD of hosts, the God of the armies of Israel, whom thou hast defied," (I Samuel 45-47).

David did not stand before Goliath in his *own* name, but in the name of the Lord. If David really wanted to get the glory, he would have went to battle with the armor of Saul. Instead, he went in God's name; therefore, he was also arrayed in *God's* armor. When we are arrayed with *God's* armor, there is no doubt that

One Stone

God has given us the victory. We might *look* overmatched and inexperienced in the sight of our enemies, but it is through our sincere *humility* that God is honored in us.

When David ran towards Goliath, he ran towards *his* destiny. Since he was armed with the armor of God, he was *more* than equipped to fulfill the plan of God. So, it is no surprise that he only needed one stone (the Word of God) to defeat the giant:

"And David put his hand in his bag, and took thence a stone, and slang it, and smote the Philistine in his forehead, that the stone sunk into his forehead; and he fell upon his face to the earth," (I Samuel 17:49).

When *we* are armed with the Word that has been hid in our hearts, and speak it to *our* giants, they have no defense against God's overwhelming power! It literally sinks into the heads of our giants, for they can not prevent the velocity of the Word from knocking them down in defeat. Our enemies are subject to us, when God's words are spoken through faith!

Goliath's fatal flaw was that he had another man carrying his shield in front of him (1 Samuel 17:41). His confidence was placed in another man to protect him from the attack of his enemy. Goliath was massive and a great champion for his people, but his trust was in what man could do for him, as well as, what he could

Break Free

do for himself. So, when the stone was slung, he was defenseless to its power, for his shield rested in the hands of a man who simply could not protect him. No man can protect a giant, just as no man can prevent us from speaking God's word to the giants that are in our lives. The spirits of this world are defenseless against the power that has been sown into our hearts, because they do not understand that God's Word is the key for us to fulfill our destiny.

~ *Destiny Fulfilled* ~

"So David prevailed over the Philistine with a sling and with a stone, and smote the Philistine, and slew him; but there was no sword in the hand of David. Therefore David ran, and stood upon the Philistine, and took his sword, and drew it out of the sheath thereof, and slew him, and cut off his head therewith. And when the Philistines saw their champion was dead, they fled. And the men of Israel and of Judah arose, and shouted, and pursued the Philistines, until thou come to the valley, and to the gates of Ekron. And the wounded of the Philistines fell down by the way to Shaaraim, even unto Gath, and unto Ekron," (I Samuel 17:50-52).

Goliath was dead, but David had to cut off the head of the giant in order to reclaim God's sheep (the children of Israel). When *we* cut off the heads of the spiritual giants that have hindered us from God and His promises, it opens the door for the remnant of God to take back what the enemy has stolen, as well as defeat

One Stone

those enemies that they have been fighting for years. When the enemy's prized champion has been defeated, they *flee*, for they are not equipped to fight against a fearless army. All we need is *one* stone to defeat our giant, and through our fearlessness we will then carry the head of that giant back to the holy city. When the people of God see our victory, they can take courage and know that God is able to defeat *any* enemy that comes their way with just *One Stone*.

≈ The Real Party ≈

"I press toward the mark for the prize of the high calling of God in Christ Jesus," (Philippians 3:14).

There is nothing like the exhilaration we feel after having seen a giant in our lives to fall and die. Our lives no longer carry the burdens and weights that had attached themselves to us, and we are now excited about our newfound freedom. We don't fully understand what happened, but we *do* know that the source of our fear has been destroyed. Still, what was the purpose of the matter? Why did it take being terrified for so long, before the "David" in *us* was unleashed to slay the giant?

We are God's chosen people and we are promised peace and comfort from our Father. Yet, every time we are about to enter into something that God has promised us, we are confronted by a *giant*. Without complete understanding of what we must do, we will continue to run back to our "tents" in fear, just like King Saul and the children of Israel.

~ *Emotionally Unstable* ~

One guarantee in life is that our feelings do not last. We live our lives on an emotional roller coaster – moved by every good and bad situation that comes our way. So much that one day we can be depressed and frustrated, and the next, we can be encouraged and motivated.

We have become so emotionally unstable, that God simply can not trust us with His treasures. If we choose to submit to the process that God takes us through to obtain the power and promises of God, then we can not allow our feelings to control our actions. We have become so accustomed and reliant on our emotions carrying us to our destiny, that when we do not "feel" the anointing on us, we are discombobulated and lose focus on moving forward in God.

~ *The Real Party* ~

It is amusing that when we are having a "Holy Ghost" party in church where everyone is shouting, speaking in tongues, crying and dancing, we attribute that to the power of God and everyone is excited about the experience. Unfortunately, when the "party" is over

Break Free

and it is time to clean up, everyone ignores the worship experience of cleansing the temple. Everyone wants to participate in the "party," but no one wants to help clean up the mess that was left from the party. It takes a faithful person to let what they just participated in, begin to cleanse, purify and change them. "Wherewithal shall a young man cleanse his way? by taking heed thereto according to thy word," (Psalms 119:9).

We cheat ourselves from so much in God when we ignore the cleaning process that the word of God wants to take us through. A party cause's chaos; it is receiving a word of revelation that completely disrupts the order of our lives to give us insight and a deeper knowledge into what God is working in us. Cleaning up brings things into order; it is the actual transformation process of being put in order, in accordance to the will of God.

Both are absolutely necessary for us to grow in our walk with God. "Order my steps in thy word: and let not any iniquity have dominion over me," (Psalms 119:133). It is time that we get tired of "party" hopping, and allow God's Word to transform us to be the ones to *throw* the "party." We are so dependent on others to inspire us and stir up our emotions, that we are ignorant to the "party" in us that just lays dormant.

The Real Party

One thing that we notice in "natural" parties and clubs is the false personas of many of the party goers. Everyone dresses in style, wears make-up, perfume, cologne, new shoes *and* new clothes. We try to look our best so that we can impress the other party goers, and draw attention to ourselves.

The same attitude, unfortunately, has infiltrated the church and we have become experts of cleaning and purifying the *outside*. We have our suits, dresses, shoes, perfumes, colognes, earrings, purses, robes, and let us not forget our emasculate bibles that look like they have *never* been opened. We do not want others to think that we are any less "anointed" than anyone else, so we learn to flawlessly carry our façades in an attempt to impress people and draw them to Christ.

In both settings, when we have a façade, we end up only drawing people that are just like us. In church, we become so caught up with our façades of "perfection" and "holiness," that we connect to people similar to us who neither have the active and living Word of God in their lives, nor the understanding of the Word. We do not know who *we* are and therefore remain stuck in the routine of just "partying."

Do not be mistaken, we *do* have a good time at the "party," but when we continue in our "regular" lives, we have nothing in us that has the ability to change our reality or perspective. Every *weekend* is the same, but during the *week*, our lives are empty of fulfillment. What will we do when our masks have to come off, and our feelings of excitement subside? What then? All we know is "partying," but where has *that* really gotten us?

There is a time in each one of our lives when "enough is enough," and we want more to life than what we have been living. The "partying" has caused chaos and wrecked havoc in our lives, and is the result of God's word not being properly sown into our hearts. Understand, however, that we will go through much chaos until we allow His word to accomplish what it was sent to do. Living our lives and wondering why we go through such hard turmoil, our questions remain void of answers because we do not understand that God's word is lethal to us when we get in the way of its intended destination – our *hearts.*

When we surrender ourselves to God, He establishes an order to our process that equips us with understanding, and will empower us to live in our divine destiny. We then can begin to live empowered by the transformation process that God takes us through. Being transformed by God's Word, we reach places in our lives where the power that has been given to us must be released for the fulfillment of His Word that we have been carrying.

≈ Pressed Through Giants ≈

Now, there are "walls" blocking us from moving closer to God. There is no way around these massive "walls," and even in all of our own strength, they can never be moved. The "walls" are our giants, and if we do not slay them, we will never see the fulfillment of the Word that God gave us.

~ Whose Report Will We Believe? ~

"And they returned from searching of the land after forty days. And they went and came to Moses, and to Aaron, and to all the congregation of the children of Israel, unto the wilderness of Paran, to Kadesh; and brought back word unto them, and unto all the congregation, and shewed them the fruit of the land. And they told him, and said, We came unto the land whither thou sentest us, and surely it floweth with milk and honey; and this is the fruit of it. Nevertheless the people be strong that dwell in the land, and the cities are walled, and very great: and **moreover we saw the children of Anak there**. The Amalekites dwell in the

Pressed through giants

land of the south: and the Hittites, and the Jebusites, and the Amorites, dwell in the mountains: and the Canaanites dwell by the sea, and by the coast of Jordan. And Caleb stilled the people before Moses, and said, Let us go up at once, and possess it; for we are well able to overcome it. But the men that went up with him said, We be not able to go up against the people; for they are stronger than we. And they brought up **an evil report of the land** which they had searched unto the children of Israel, saying, The land, through which we have gone to search it, is a land that eateth up the inhabitants thereof; and all the people that we saw in it are men of a great stature. And there **we saw the giants**, the sons of Anak, which come of the giants: and **we were in our own sight as grasshoppers**, and so we were in their sight," (Numbers 13:25-33).

Moses led the children of Israel through the wilderness, where they made many mistakes, but God was merciful and forgave them in spite of their attitudes and sinful habits. When they finally reached the brink of their journey and were about to enter into their promised land, they sent twelve spies to search out the land. After forty days, the spies came back with reports of the great land and the abundant resources that occupied the land. Nevertheless, only Caleb and Joshua came back with a positive report of all they had seen. The other ten spies ruined the prospects of entering into their promised land, for they saw and were threatened by the sons of Anak who were currently dwelling in the land.

Break Free

They saw *giants*, and no matter how good the land and its resources looked, they could not see past the giants that blocked them from their destiny. They lost hope; so instead of *inspiring* the children of Israel, they *discouraged* them to become fearful of giants that the rest of the children of Israel had not even seen. God had brought them through the Red sea, He had given them food and water in a dry place, He healed the waters, and He guided them by His presence. Despite all of this, the people forgot the works of God and became fearful of their giants, through *one* bad report. Whose report will *we* believe?

The ten spies with a *bad* report did not lie to the children of Israel, for it was a fact that there were giants in the land. However, their report was *natural*, for it dealt with the facts of what they *saw*, instead of the powerful and faithful God that continued to lead them. God had done marvelous things for His chosen people, but they refused to believe that He was going to give them their land in the face of those giants. So, for their unbelief, God cursed the people of Israel to wander in the wilderness for forty years; one year for everyday that the promise land was searched out. Through unbelief, they sentenced themselves to a state of wandering, and never partook of the goodness that was intended for them to possess. Even after receiving their sentence from God, many of them became angry instead of repenting, and tried to conquer the land in their *own* strength. However, they were defeated for their efforts.

Just like the children of Israel, we have to decide whose report *we* will believe. Are we going to press through our giant or are we going to be sentenced to a life of mediocrity? The children of Israel still received many blessings from God in the wilderness, but they did not cross over into their promised land. In our lives, *we* have been set free from our "Egypt" and led forth by the guidance of God. We have seen many miracles occur through the Word that He placed in us, and we eventually come to the place of crossing over into *our* "promised land." It is imperative that we don't take our eyes off of God, despite whatever is trying to block our vision from seeing the benefits of pressing into our destiny.

~ Land of Giants ~

We have been led by the Spirit into the land of giants; however, there is no way for us to live in this abundant and fruitful land without faith in God. In this land, the deeper we travel, the greater we need to rest in our faith in God.

"And now, behold, the LORD hath kept me alive, as he said, these forty and five years, even since the LORD spake this word unto Moses, while the children of Israel wandered in the wilderness: and now,

Break Free

lo, I am this day fourscore and five years old. As yet I am as strong this day as I was in the day that Moses sent me: as my strength was then, even so is my strength now, for war, both to go out, and to come in. Now therefore give me this mountain, whereof the LORD spake in that day; for thou heardest in that day how the Anakims were there, and that the cities were great and fenced: if so be the LORD will be with me, then I shall be able to drive them out, as the LORD said," (Joshua 14:10-12).

For forty five years, Caleb waited for his opportunity to conquer the land God promised him; although he had faith that God would take the children of Israel in victory to the land of Canaan from the beginning. He had to wait forty five years to demonstrate the action of his faith. God has given each of us an individual measure of faith that is more than enough to conquer the territory that is promised to us. "And Caleb drove thence the three sons of Anak, Sheshai, and Ahiman, and Talmai, the children of Anak," (Joshua 15:14).

In the battle of David and Goliath, we can see the similarity of character with their ancestors, the children of Israel and the sons of Anak. One thing we must realize is that when we do not slay our spiritual giants, we place the same burden to fight those giants on the generations to follow. If Israel would have faced their fears in the wilderness, Goliath would have never been born. God is now conditioning a nation that will

Pressed through giants

no longer be afraid to obtain a greater life in Him, despite the challenges they will face.

~ *The Giant of Gath* ~

Goliath's home city was called *Gath*, meaning "wine press," and he was the champion of the Philistines. So, this giant that presented himself before Israel was there to press them into "wine." God has created giants, like Goliath, in our lives for the sole purpose of pressing the best out of *us*. Israel did not understand that it was their divine destiny to be pressed by Goliath in order to be transformed from "grapes" to "wine." When *we* avoid the "wine press," like the children of Israel, we avoid the opportunity to be changed from our natural state of mind to a spiritual state of understanding our God.

Nevertheless, through David, God was able to receive the glory that He originally wanted to receive in the wilderness with the children of Israel. Every giant that we face is purposed to "press" us to a higher spiritual level after we have defeated them in battle. When David defeated Goliath, he took the sword of the giant (his power), and cut off Goliath's head. When we have defeated *our* giants, in the power of God's word, we strip our giants of their weapons that have controlled the territory, and we render the enemy powerless. We have gained a greater understanding of the tricks of our enemy, and are no longer afraid of what we must do to overcome them.

~ *Challenged to Overcome* ~

We have carried the power of God to the battlefield to face our giant, and it is essential that we embrace the opportunity to accomplish what the Word in us was initially sent to do. Only through unwavering faith in God's power will we see our giants defeated, although many times we choose to stand on *uncertainty*, instead of faith. It is because, deep down in our hearts, we are unsure if God is going to do what we have been praying for Him to do.

For us to achieve victory, we have to trust God in spite of our overwhelming circumstances. Even if we have not yet faced the giant, our faith is in God, not the situation. God is not moved by giants, He is moved by the faith that we have in His Word. The power of God's word, when spoken in *faith*, supersedes the challenge of any spirit or person that has come against us, and in its appointed time, every word that has been sown in us will be challenged by a giant. It is our choice, however, to allow that desperate situation to press us and transform our faith into reality.

It is God's perfect will for us to reap every blessing that is connected to His word. He wants our

Pressed through giants

faith to lead us to many spiritual and natural blessings as we experience His word coming alive through our faith; but when we doubt, we allow curses into our lives that can only be broken when the giants have been slain. We will live defeated when we doubt the power of God's Word and His ability to defeat our enemies. Furthermore, we will never see the fulfillment of God's Word and His promises, until we are *pressed* to slay our giants through faith in Jesus Christ.

PART TWO:

"RECEIVING OUR REWARD"

≈Abiding in Christ≈

Do we *fully* understand the depth to abiding in God? We proclaim that we are abiding in Christ, but have no evidence at all, of His presence working through our lives. We have associated being faithful to our church responsibilities as "abiding in Christ," and we have labeled our lives as "holy" because of all the things that we have given up or resisted. One question must be answered though, "If we are abiding in Christ, why are none of His words being fulfilled in our lives?" "If ye abide in me, and my words abide in you, ye shall ask what ye will, and it shall be done unto you," (John 15:7). The Word tells us to ask what we will, but we often lack understanding of what Jesus was really trying to teach us.

"I am the true vine, and my Father is the husbandman. Every branch in me that beareth not fruit he taketh away: and every branch that beareth fruit, **he purgeth it**, that it may bring forth more fruit. Now ye are clean through the word which I have spoken unto you. Abide in me, and I in you. As the branch cannot bear fruit of itself, except it abide in the vine; no more can ye, except ye abide in me. I am the vine, ye are the branches: He that abideth in me, and I in him, the same bringeth forth much fruit: for without me ye can do nothing." (John 15:1-5)

Jesus – the Word of God – is the *true* vine and we are the branches that are connected to Him. When we bear some fruit of our connection to the Vine, the Spirit of God purges us so that we can bear even *more* "fruit." Nothing that we bear is produced from *us*, but from the Spirit; through our connection to His Word, fruit is produced through us. When we abide in the Word, we are purged and become clean, which enables His Spirit to flow through us and produce fruit for those in need.

~ *The Hindering Spirit of "Self"* ~

In today's society we see plenty of people in need, but very few results of those needs being met. What is plugging the flow of God from reaching the needs of His people? It is our self-image that has prevented the power of God from satisfying the insufficiencies of the needy. Our self-image has not allowed us to look past our own needs to consider another's. It is the reason why someone else's victory is not being manifested in their life.

Break Free

We are attached to the word of God, but we are too busy satisfying our *own* needs to allow the standard of God to venture into the lives of the people we are ordained to reach. The power of God has never left His Word; it is just that we have prevented it from reaching its intended destination. The more we "feast" and partake of the Word of God, the "fatter" we get; and without releasing it to our neighbors, the more slothful and content we become.

~ The Gift of Release ~

We are destroying ourselves without even knowing it; subtly killing ourselves by not exercising the gift of *release.* When we eat food and receive it into our bodies, the food provides us with energy and nutrients that strengthen us. As the food travels through our body, it reaches a point where it has performed its purpose in us, and what is left, has to be released out of us.

If not released, the excess becomes toxic to our bodies, and if we are not careful, it will kill us. The word is the same. When we receive the Word, it flows through our bodies and transforms us, conditions us, and renews the Spirit within us. The Word, though, is not intended to *stay* in our bodies. It has planted and performed a great work in *us*, but in order to manifest

Abiding in Christ

results for someone else as well, we *must* release that Word.

When we release God's word, our hearts are opened to be filled with *new* Word. It is the transformation process of an "eater," becoming a "sower." The "sower" always has seed, but the "eater" is never satisfied. We grow up hearing it is better to give than it is to receive (Acts 20:35), and it is a truth that many of us neither understand, nor carry out. It is our responsibility to sow God's Word into others, but sometimes we are afraid to let go of it because we are unsure of the next time we will "eat." Our connection to the word of God can either strengthen us, or destroy us, but it is *our* choice.

When will we get tired of ourselves so that others may see *Christ* through us? When we surrender to the purging of God, He consumes our image so that only the image of *God* remains. No matter what is burned in the fire, the loss is necessary in order to be reconnected with the image we were created to be. Our ambitions, goals, desires, preferences, and comfort zones are all consumed so that God's purpose, assignment and destiny can be made alive in us. If we are to abide in God, we can not avoid the fire, for it is our divine appointment to be consumed by the Spirit of the Living God.

Break Free

God has sown a "seed" into our hearts which transforms into a "fruit" that contains even *more* "seeds" inside of it. When people consume the "fruit" that we bear, they have received "seeds." It is then their decision as to what they will do with those "seeds." Do not forget that it is *our* responsibility to be yielded to the Spirit of God, so that fruit may be produced through us.

~ *Fallen Branches* ~

One day I was cutting the grass around a fruit tree on our church's property. While I was cutting, I had to move some branches that had fallen off the fruit tree during a vicious wind storm that had come through. I noticed that there was still fruit attached to the stems of the branches. The branches had been producing fruit and performing their functions, but still broke off from the tree when the storm came.

Many of *us* have become like those fallen branches. We walk in obedience to what the Spirit of God is calling us to do, but become too attached to the "fruit" that we have produced. We do not want to release the "fruit" because we are too proud of what God has allowed us accomplish. We are so fixated on the success that our obedience brings that we take our eyes off the power source. So, when the wind vehemently blows in our lives, and it is time for the "fruit" to be released, the weight of it pulls us down and we are broken off from the "Tree of Life" that sustains us.

Anytime we live in the past – good *and* bad experiences – and hold on to what God has ordained for us to release, it becomes a *burden*. Which, when given the right amount of pressure, and the storm comes, it weighs on us and severs our fellowship with God and our connection to His power. When we weaken our connection to the Spirit, we *and* our fruit become vulnerable to being disregarded as waste. We are then of no use and become an eyesore to all that see us. We must daily seek God and His righteousness in all things to avoid becoming comfortable in where we are, for we do not want to be left defenseless and destroyed by a storm that was sent to *strengthen* our connection to God.

~ How Bad Do You Want It? ~

We want to abide in God and live in our purpose in Him, but we often face apprehension and fear. Be strong and know that it is natural for us to have fears. There is not *one* person that has not been struck with fear in some sort of way. The very importance of our trials and tribulations are to draw us out of our natural state of fear, to a spiritual state of rest in the Master's hands. Will we stick close to God when He leads us into persecution and suffering? Or will we withdraw ourselves from God and remain in our natural state?

It is easy to abide in something when we are void of distress and afflictions, but our true desires and character are measured in the midst of afflictions. Why are we so afraid to lose our natural lives? How have they *really* benefited us? To trust God when our natural senses say it is impossible is a true revelation of our faith in Him.

God has repeatedly asked me, "How bad do you want it?" No matter what I desire, the question is *always* the same. To abide in God and receive His promises requires patience and endurance. "And so, after he had patiently endured, he obtained the promise," (Hebrews 6:15). One of the most grueling processes a believer can go through is when he or she is learning *endurance*. It is a quality that, at the end of our journey, requires pressing toward the reward, in spite of the obstacles that we may see ahead. In victory we claim; our deliverance, our healing, and our salvation but it can only be obtained through the process of enduring. We must understand that endurance is not being passive and lethargic, but rather, it is the act of withstanding afflictions so that we can be empowered through our journey.

Abiding in Christ

In my junior year in high school, we were completing the football season. One of my problems that season was that at the end of each game, I would be tired and have absolutely no energy. So, when spring came around, I joined the track team to build my endurance for the upcoming football season. I was fast and could have competed in the short sprints like some of my football buddies, but I committed myself to running long-distance races. That means that I was separated from my teammates, but all in an effort to be well conditioned for the upcoming football season.

I was bigger than all of the long distance runners and was completely out of my comfort zone. Nevertheless, whenever we commit ourselves in *anything* to obtain endurance, we will be humbled. Every race that I ran, I lost by a *huge* margin. It was not comforting that I was all *alone* on the track, but the only thing that kept me going was the reward of gaining the endurance I needed for football. My body and my mind would always tell me to quit; that I was embarrassing myself, and was wasting my time, but something inside of me kept pushing me to the finish line of each race.

Another way I was conditioning myself was by weight training. So many days on the track I had no energy or strength to go on, but I *did*. I had to endure my teammates, my coaches, and my friends laughing at each of my lost races, and I endured so much rejection from people who were embarrassed at my "poor" performances. No one understood why I was subjecting myself to such "suffering," but they did not realize that I had to go through the losses, the jeers, and the rejection, in order to receive strength, endurance and dominance for the new football season that was to come. It is *our* endurance that keeps us in the presence of God, while also carrying us to His promises.

~ Before Domination, There Is Humiliation ~

"By humility and the fear of the LORD are riches, and honour, and life," (Proverbs 22:4).

We all want to be dominant and victorious in our lives, but few of us are willing to endure the suffering required to obtain such power. Before *domination*, there is *humiliation*. Jesus' disciples could not cast out an evil spirit from a desperate boy. After *Jesus* rebuked the evil spirit, the disciples asked, "Why couldn't *we* do that?" Today, so many of us, too, are asking Jesus the *same* question. Jesus always has a simple response: "Howbeit this kind goeth not out but by prayer and fasting," (Matthew 17:21). We want God to endow us with *great* power that will render the enemy defenseless, but we choose not to endure anything that will gain such results.

Abiding in Christ

God requires us to "exercise" our faith in Him. It is because of our trials and tribulations pressing against us, that our faith (our muscles) can be revealed. One thing you realize when you begin to "exercise" is that most people are not with you in the "gym." "For many are called, but few are chosen," (Matthew 22:14). It is those individuals who have taken aim on their destiny and have grabbed a hold of purpose, that continue to "exercise," despite the fact that they do not see *immediate* results. They know and trust that when it is time to perform, they are prepared for victory, for their faith has already been tried. The battles they face are then, just a "stepping stone" to the manifestation of what they have been working towards.

Everything we need is inside of us, and the pressures we endure are what help to determine what will ultimately come out of us. We must decide not to let anything separate us from abiding in the presence of God. "For I am persuaded, that neither death, nor life, nor angels, nor principalities, nor powers, nor things present, nor things to come, Nor height, nor depth, nor any other creature, shall be able to separate us from the love of God, which is in Christ Jesus our Lord," (Romans 8:38-39).

An angel of God spoke to Paul on his way to Rome, and told him fear not, for his journey in the ship was not his end *(Acts 27:23-25)*. The Word that Paul

Break Free

heard did not change the stormy environment, but he – even though he was a *prisoner* – had to hold on to that Word in spite of the chaos that was presented before him. If Paul had not been on the ship, the other people probably would have abandoned the ship and died in their ignorance (*they* had no Word).

Sometimes our captivity, even the pressures of life, is necessary for others who are ignorant to God, to be delivered. When we complain and get frustrated, we block the avenues that God has set up for us to receive a word that can free others as well. There is no hope where there is no Word, and we also are hopeless when we do not hold on to the Word that is ordained to bring hope to the lost.

God had a Word to deliver to Rome and no circumstance presented was going to prevent the message from being delivered. With every Word from Him, there is life; we carry life to the lifeless. It is our role to endure the storm, no matter if the ship is destroyed or how high the waves get in the sea, we must be determined in our minds to abide in the plan of God.

~ Bound to Liberate ~

"And the multitude rose up together against them: and the magistrates rent off their clothes, and commanded to beat them. And when they had laid many

Abiding in Christ

stripes upon them, they cast them into prison, charging the jailor to keep them safely: Who, having received such a charge, thrust them into the inner prison, and made their feet fast in the stocks. And at midnight Paul and Silas prayed, and sang praises unto God: and the prisoners heard them. And suddenly there was a great earthquake, so that the foundations of the prison were shaken: and immediately all the doors were opened, and every one's bands were loosed. And the keeper of the prison awaking out of his sleep, and seeing the prison doors open, he drew out his sword, and would have killed himself, supposing that the prisoners had been fled. But Paul cried with a loud voice, saying, Do thyself no harm: for we are all here. Then he called for a light, and sprang in, and came trembling, and fell down before Paul and Silas, And brought them out, and said, Sirs, what must I do to be saved? And they said, Believe on the Lord Jesus Christ, and thou shalt be saved, and thy house. And they spake unto him the word of the Lord, and to all that were in his house. And he took them the same hour of the night, and washed their stripes; and was baptized, he and all his, straightway," (Acts 16:22-33).

In spite of Paul and Silas' predicament, being beaten and thrown in jail, they began to praise God and glorify His name. In their captivity, they looked to God and He freed them from their prison and binds. What is amazing is that they did not leave. In spite of being set free, they remained in their captivity.

Break Free

If Paul and Silas would have left, when the keeper of the prison came and saw that the prisoners were free, he would have committed suicide. *Instead*, the keeper heard the call of Paul, laid down his sword, and fell down before Paul and Silas as a broken man. He was the keeper of the prison and had been the only free man, but in that moment he realized that is was *him* who was truly held captive.

How many times do we hesitate or reject hearing from God and flee *our* captivity at the moment He releases the binds from *us*? How many of us are willing to wait in captivity so that others who are captive and lost can be saved? Are we willing to witness to the very person that beat us and threw us in prison? It is up to us if we want to see families transformed and saved. Paul and Silas were placed in prison for the sole purpose of breaking the curse of sin in that prison keeper's family. When *we* take our focus off of *our* situation and focus on God, many will come running to us asking, "What must I do to be saved?" When God is through, the same person that beat *you* will be the same one mending those same stripes.

~ *The Unity of Abiding In Christ* ~

When we first receive Jesus Christ as our Lord and Savoir, the trials and sufferings we go through for the Word's sake are not "advertised" in the "brochure."

Abiding in Christ

Who would want to volunteer for such suffering and persecution anyway? Once we receive a Word that is alive in our bones, it does not matter what we go through. "But he that shall endure unto the end, the same shall be saved," (Matthew 24:13). The Word is too valuable to let go for the temporary gratification that the world brings.

The purpose for the Word being sown in us is for it to bear fruit for our neighbor. Though God's Word is always the same, we carry a different perspective of it than others because its use is uniquely fit for the individual role we hold in the body of Christ. "From whom the whole body fitly joined together and compacted by that which every joint supplieth, according to the effectual working in the measure of every part, maketh increase of the body unto the edifying of itself in love." (Ephesians 4:16)

We need each "body part" to carry their perspective to whomever they are connected to, so that the whole body of Christ can be edified and nourished in unity for the will of God. The Word must abide in me if I am to carry "fruit" to the people that I am connected to. If there is discord, the whole "body" suffers because of the lack of "fruit" being produced through *one* transient "body part."

Break Free

When we place our neighbor's well being before ours, it opens the door to the unlimited power of God to flow through us and exceed the need of our neighbor. "This is my commandment, That ye love one another, as I have loved you. Greater love hath no man than this, that a man lay down his life for his friends," (John 15:12-13). It is not until we are ready and willing to lose our lives for others, that the move of God is manifested through us. Then will it not only benefit us and our neighbor, but also anyone else "connected" to a "fruit-bearing" part.

~ *Handled with Care* ~

When I worked in a warehouse, I had the job of receiving in new shipments. In my duties, I had to first unload the truck until it was empty and separate the product according to the differences in materials or colors, next. Then, I had to verify if we received the correct product. Finally, I had to transport the product to the store preparation area so that the product could be shipped to the stores. If I did not complete my duties effectively and proficiently, it caused delays for the next department. It was only when I handled my responsibilities, that the next department was enabled to run effectively.

God has gathered us to do a mighty work in Him. We must follow through on what our duties are so that whoever we carry it to, receives what they need so they can release it to the next person. When we walk in grace, it is not going to be easy unloading the weights we have been carrying, and it is even harder to separate the things that are contrary to one another. We may even have some sleepless nights when we begin to verify the truth about ourselves. Regardless, it is all necessary and worth it in the end when we have the opportunity to carry a refined treasure to our neighbor that is in desperate need of it. When we regard the big picture and where we fit in the body, it will change our hearts to surrender and be able to carry God's grace to the people we are connected to.

≈ Living in the Grace of God ≈

"For the law was given by Moses, but grace and truth came by Jesus Christ," (John 1:17).

Grace is more than a prayer given over a meal. It is more than just a witty phrase recited in the ears of unbelievers; it is the essence of our being. Without grace, we are doomed to destruction, for it is the key to our salvation. The problem is that we do not understand what grace *is*. We can not receive grace unless we are honest in our hearts and confess that we need it.

Unfortunately, some of us frustrate and reject the grace of God (Gal 2:21). We have perfected our spiritual "routine" *so* much, that our prayers have lost passion, our memory verses have diluted their power, and our churches have allowed sincerity to be replaced with entertainment. We "know" so much, that our lives become controlled by the lifestyle that we have created,

Living in the Grace of God

and we live our lives void of genuine grace, creating our own "holding cells."

~ *Grace Is* ~

"And he said unto me, My grace is sufficient for thee: for my strength is made perfect in weakness. Most gladly therefore will I rather glory in my infirmities, that the power of Christ may rest upon me." (II Corinthians 12:9)

Grace is not preparing a life altering sermon or writing a well-organized and thought-provoking book. It is not something that we can create in our own strength. It is laying our lives, thoughts, dreams, hearts, and gifts on the line for the edifying of others. It is taking full responsibility for the actions of *others*. It is suffering in your insufficiency so that others may be unburdened. Jesus Christ paid off *our* debt, when He suffered and died on the cross. Will we lay down *our* lives to see the yoke on the burdened destroyed?

The anointing is resting in the arms of grace. Where grace is, people are being delivered from addictions, saved from lives of sin and corruption, and freed from their vain self-images. We are the chosen vessels that have been sent to carry grace to a world that so desperately needs it.

Break Free

Grace is free and abundant so it is not limited by status, but rather, it is given according to the size of the void in the recipient (Ephesians 4:16). Our vessels are filled, according to the needs of the people that we are ordained to reach. "For by grace are ye saved through faith; and that not of yourselves: it is the gift of God: Not of works, lest any man should boast. For we are his workmanship, created in Christ Jesus unto good works, which God hath before ordained that we should walk in them," (Ephesians 2:8-10).

It is not *our* words that save, it is *grace* that saves. It is not our knowledge that renews a mind, it is *grace* that renews. Nothing we do can justify our lives; it is only through grace that we are pleasing in the sight of God. When we make up in our minds that we cannot save ourselves *or* others, but by the grace of God, we will then quit trying so hard and allow God to transform us into His image. Our lives will be freed from the bondage of trying to fulfill our destiny through the law, and we will walk in the power of grace.

~ Sharing Grace ~

We open our hearts to receive the grace of God, but are unwilling to *show* His grace to those that need it in their lives. God has acquitted all the charges that we were guilty of when we received him into our hearts. Who are *we* to consider someone unworthy of God's

Living in the Grace of God

grace? We have forgotten the pits that had us enslaved to the desires of our flesh. Regardless, we can not be selective to whom God wants to give grace to. We, unfortunately, block God's grace from reaching a world so desperately in need of it, while placing strongholds around us so we can not be hurt.

If someone makes a mistake in the church, they are treated like a leper and separated. While still stuck in their mess, they are openly humiliated by the vicious looks they receive and whispers that they hear. No matter how many years have passed after their mistake, there is still an "invisible" label on them.

Where is *Jesus* in our churches? Did Christ condemn? We arrogantly mistreat them this way, but when *our* "mess" is brought to the light, we become upset by how we are similarly being treated. We can not live as hypocrites anymore, because if it was not for the grace of God, daily washing away the mistakes in *our* lives, we would be saturated in the "stench" of our filthiness.

We are undeserving of the grace of God, but He still fills us with it everyday. When we sow grace into the lives of people that have done evil things to us, or others, it enables us to abundantly receive God's grace into *our* lives. We can not let the feelings of hatred and bitterness, corrupt our lives. Sadly, others may never apologize, or even show a hint of remorse for what they do. However, if we are influenced by their actions, our emotions will place them up as "idols" in our lives.

We, then, will be completely separated from God, because we will not be able to see past those "idols." Whatever the circumstance may be, *they* are not our enemy. Our *true* enemy continues to use our past to distort our focus from the power of God that liberates us from the scars of those past experiences. If our spiritual enemy can keep us restless and preoccupied, we can never present the Gospel of Peace to those in need.

"And being found in fashion as a man, he humbled himself, and became obedient unto death, even the death of the cross," (Philippians 2:8). Jesus was obedient, *even* unto death, in order to bring salvation to a world that was and is still covered in sin. Thankfully, there are great qualities in all of us that can be used to reach out to the world. We can not withhold the greatness of the Word, because of those that have mistreated or hurt us, for someone is depending on the grace and the power inside of us to help to liberate *them*.

~ Loving Our Enemies ~

"But I say unto you, Love your enemies, bless them that curse you, do good to them that hate you, and

Living in the Grace of God

pray for them which despitefully use you, and persecute you," (Matthew 5:44).

I once had a boss that did not like me at all. I never did *anything* to him, but since my friends were on his "bad side," I was lumped into the same lot with them. I could not understand why he mistreated me. I always got the "short end of the stick," and never was promoted despite all of my hard work. No matter how hard I worked, he continued to try and find a way to fire me. Others also took notice to how he was treating me, and contrary to their advice, I kept working without even complaining to my boss once. I treated him with respect despite all that was said and done to me.

By the time he transferred to supervise another department, he had to accept the person that I truly was and *not* the person he had stereotyped me to be. Whatever the world does to us only affects us negatively when we *receive* their condemnation. "There is therefore now no condemnation to them which are in Christ Jesus, who walk not after the flesh, but after the Spirit," (Romans 8:1). If I would have acted like he wanted me to, he would have been able to justify his actions and feelings about me. However, by living free from his stereotypes, the door was opened for him to receive something he did not deserve: *grace*.

Break Free

When we show grace to an undeserving recipient, God showers us with His immeasurable favor in the sight of an unholy world. To deny grace to others is to deny His favor being manifested in us, in the presence of unbelievers. There has to be a difference in how we carry ourselves in this world, and the basis is living in the grace of God. The longer we live, the more grace we need to combat all the giants that are lined up to keep us from the blessings of God.

"Then they cried out with a loud voice, and stopped their ears, and ran upon him with one accord, And cast him out of the city, and stoned him: and the witnesses laid down their clothes at a young man's feet, whose name was Saul. And they stoned Stephen, calling upon God, and saying, Lord Jesus, receive my spirit. And he kneeled down, and cried with a loud voice, Lord, lay not this sin to their charge. And when he had said this, he fell asleep," (Acts 7:57-60).

Stephen was professing the testimony of God to the His people, and instead of being pricked in their hearts by his powerful words, they were *offended* by the message and chose to stone him. Nevertheless, in the midst of this violent act, Stephen pleaded for God to forgive those people for their ignorance. He could have cried for God to destroy them right where they stood, but the grace in his heart desired for them to receive the love of God in spite of their wrong.

Living in the Grace of God

~ *A Humble Giver of Grace* ~

The apostles of the early church suffered many persecutions, imprisonments and martyrdom, *all* for the cause of spreading the gospel of grace to the lost. When God's grace is in us, it does not matter what opposition may come our way, for we know that God's grace will conquer the hearts of the unbelievers. "For God, who commanded the light to shine out of darkness, hath shined in our hearts, to give the light of the knowledge of the glory of God in the face of Jesus Christ," (II Corinthians 4:6). God desires to equip us for our journey in Him and fill us with His grace, so that His compassion can shine forth through us and transform the lives of His creation.

David found himself in the "valley of uncertainty" after he killed Goliath. He began to ascend up the social "ladder" in the kingdom of Israel, and found favor in the sight of the king and the people of Israel. When all seemed to be going well for David, King Saul overheard the praises that David was receiving from the people of his kingdom. Saul became jealous and full of hatred, which led to a chain of events that left David fleeing for his life. Though Saul constantly pursued after David, David never let the situation corrupt his heart towards the anointed king of Israel.

Break Free

"Then Saul took three thousand chosen men out of all Israel, and went to seek David and his men upon the rocks of the wild goats. And he came to the sheepcotes by the way, where was a cave; and Saul went in to cover his feet: and David and his men remained in the sides of the cave. And the men of David said unto him, Behold the day of which the LORD said unto thee, Behold, I will deliver thine enemy into thine hand, that thou mayest do to him as it shall seem good unto thee. Then David arose, and cut off the skirt of Saul's robe privily. And it came to pass afterward, that David's heart smote him, because he had cut off Saul's skirt. And he said unto his men, The LORD forbid that I should do this thing unto my master, the LORD's anointed, to stretch forth mine hand against him, seeing he is the anointed of the LORD. So David stayed his servants with these words, and suffered them not to rise against Saul. But Saul rose up out of the cave, and went on his way. David also arose afterward, and went out of the cave, and cried after Saul, saying, My lord the king. And when Saul looked behind him, David stooped with his face to the earth, and bowed himself," (I Samuel 24:2-8).

David did not understand what he had done to provoke Saul, yet he remained respectful, despite the king's numerous attempts to kill him. David refused to use his relationship with God to bring Saul to repentance. He did not feel the need to "capture" the throne that he was already anointed to fill; he just waited, humbly, for *God* to move in his life.

Living in the Grace of God

In the midst of a cave, David and his men hid from the king, only to have Saul fall right into their hands for certain victory. David's men advised him to seize the moment and kill Saul, for God created the opportunity for David. Much to their surprise, David refused to strike down God's anointed. He showed mercy to the king by not killing him, but more importantly, he showed grace by being kind to a man that was undeserving of it.

David *had* to be tired of wandering from place to place, but he did not allow his circumstance to distort his perspective of what God wanted. Contrary to what his men thought, it was not David's time to be king, and instead of forcing himself into his ordained position he followed the grace of God to ascend to the throne of Israel.

"And it came to pass, when David had made an end of speaking these words unto Saul, that Saul said, Is this thy voice, my son David? And Saul lifted up his voice, and wept. And he said to David, Thou art more righteous than I: for thou hast rewarded me good, whereas I have rewarded thee evil. And thou hast shewed this day how that thou hast dealt well with me: forasmuch as when the LORD had delivered me into thine hand, thou killedst me not. For if a man find his enemy, will he let him go well away? wherefore the LORD reward thee good for that thou hast done unto me this day. And now, behold, I know well that thou shalt surely be king, and that the kingdom of Israel shall be established in thine hand." (I Samuel 24:16-20)

Even *Saul* had to confess his wrong as David continually showed him kindness. An evil spirit dwelt in Saul's heart, and it was only through the love and mercy shown by David, that Saul saw the corruption of his own actions (I Samuel 26:21). Only through a man filled with grace, was another man that had been filled with jealousy and hatred, provoked to repent. "Then Saul said to David, Blessed be thou, my son David: thou shalt both do great things, and also shalt still prevail. So David went on his way, and Saul returned to his place," (I Samuel 26:25).

When we receive the grace of God, we are turned from ourselves and led forth to a people that have lost their way. We are no longer settled in what we can do for ourselves, but committed to receiving the same transforming power of God's grace that will lead the lost back into His arms. We are then, elevated to a freedom of living that is unknown to the natural man; a life where we are above our situations, our weaknesses, our uncertainties, and our fears. We are not bound by religion, tradition, or the letter of the law.

We are free to live and it pricks them to live in the same freedom. There is no blueprints to grace it is new everyday. We are not limited by past experiences,

Living in the Grace of God

or philosophies but the encompassing freedom of His grace.

~ *Living Above the Law* ~

"And hath raised us up together, and made us sit together in heavenly places in Christ Jesus:" (Ephesians 2:6). We are seated in heavenly places that, to the natural eye are crazy, but to the spiritual man is destiny.

"What shall we say then? Shall we continue in sin, that grace may abound? God forbid. How shall we, that are dead to sin, live any longer therein? Know ye not, that so many of us as were baptized into Jesus Christ were baptized into his death? Therefore we are buried with him by baptism into death: that like as Christ was raised up from the dead by the glory of the Father, even so we also should walk in newness of life. For if we have been planted together in the likeness of his death, we shall be also in the likeness of his resurrection: Knowing this, that our old man is crucified with him, that the body of sin might be destroyed, that henceforth we should not serve sin. For he that is dead is freed from sin. Now if we be dead with Christ, we believe that we shall also live with him: Knowing that Christ being raised from the dead dieth no more; death hath no more dominion over him. For in that he died, he died unto sin once: but in that he liveth, he liveth unto God," (Romans 6:1-10).

We are destined to live. Grace does not mean that we can do what we want; it means that we are guided by God to walk on the foundations of His Word. If we are to bring life to the lifeless, we must *walk* on the Word, not be in *bondage* to the Word. We can not obtain freedom through obligation and regulation, for they shackle us. Freedom, on the other hand, comes from the enlightenment of the knowledge of God through grace. Everything we experience is for us to come to a better understanding of the power of God's Word. Our experiences are not to shackle us in guilt and shame, but to draw us closer to the One that can redeem us from ourselves. We are created, chosen, ordained, redeemed and empowered all by His Love. It is in His love that we capture the heart of grace.

≈ Running the Race ≈

"Wherefore seeing we also are compassed about with so great a cloud of witnesses, let us lay aside every weight, and the sin which doth so easily beset us, and let us run with patience the race that is set before us," (Hebrews 12:1).

Each one of us has been assigned a "race" to run. It is imperative that we focus on our *own* "race" and not be swayed. Many believers have never even begun the "race," for they are still carrying burdens and "weights" that God has ordained to be released. When we walk in grace the burdens that we have been carrying have been lifted off our lives. God has freed us from ourselves, but now we must ensure that we remain free. The enemy wants to take away our freedom by distracting us from pursuing after our divine purpose, and whatever he can use to knock us out of alignment from the will of God, he *will* use.

Running the Race

~ *The Deception of "Weights"* ~

What is your weight? Not the measure of your body mass; what are the things in your life that are subtly disrupting you from your fellowship with God? We must be aware of what our weights are, if we are to be victorious in our "race" to a closer relationship with God. We can not allow the enemy to deceive us by these "weights" that he wants us to carry. Our "weights" are not sin, but rather, things that are of no particular use for the plan of God in our lives.

They may be sports, food, internet, television, friends, politics, the economy, movies, insecurities, feelings of inadequacy for God's use, loneliness, negativity, or even evil looks. Whatever they may be, we have to identify them and allow God to release these strongholds from our lives. If we are carrying *one* "weight," it is only a matter of time before we pick up and carry another one, and then another one, and so on. For when the storms of life run rampant in our lives and knock us off balance, we receive another "weight" to try and stabilize ourselves.

No one wants to be in lack of anything, so money may be a "weight" that we are carrying. So, if we go through a financial famine and see our finances deplete, we will look for something else to fill the void of our lack. We may get credit cards, mortgages, and loans, but they do not solve the problem, they only *add* more weight to what we are already carrying. Then we cry out to God, only when our "weights" have become so heavy, that they are *now* a burden. This is a common mistake that many of us have to eradicate from our lives because it continues to strip us of our freedom.

~ *The "Weightless" Life* ~

"Come unto me, all ye that labour and are heavy laden, and I will give you rest. Take my yoke upon you, and learn of me; for I am meek and lowly in heart: and ye shall find rest unto your souls. For my yoke is easy, and my burden is light," (Matthew 11:28-30).

We are accustomed to crying out to God when our "weights" become a heavy burden. This cycle relates back to when we were in the "world." When Jesus released us from the sins and burdens that we were carrying, He took them *all* from us. We were so accustomed to carrying them, that to be without the "weights," and to live in a newness of life, requires for us to be in constant fellowship with God. For when trials and persecution come, if we are not in communion with God, we revert back to our old ways of handling our lives. The more that *we* handle things, the heavier the load becomes. Then we become aware of our need for God, and again, cry out for His help.

Running the Race

God desires for us to live a "weightless" life. We all have to endure persecution, trials, and tribulations, but we do *not* have to accept the "weights" that are presented along with them. It is hard to endure a trial and not lean on someone or something that, while in the midst of the storm, has been conveniently placed in front of us. We have to endure and not yield to those temptations, for what we have *inside* of us, is of greater value than what has been placed in *front* of us.

How do we resist the weights that tempt us from enduring our trials? God gives us a way of escape through His Word. His Word is the key to liberating us and remaining "weightless" in spite the circumstances that we go through. Many of us are living in some sort of famine in our lives, and whatever the lack may be, without a Word from the Lord to sustain us in the midst of our lack, we will not overcome the famine. His Word is our assurance that what we are in, is for our good. To be "weightless," we have to be full of the Word. It is only through the power of God's Word that we can see the "weights" in our lives lifted off of us.

~ Overcoming "Weights" ~

A few years back, I was committed to many things, which ultimately became my "weights." I was committed to my positions in church, raising my children, working on my business, and doing all the

Break Free

things that I felt God wanted me to do. When tests and trials came, I would get frustrated in those same positions at a church. I also would show no mercy to my children *and* be completely stressed out in regards to my business. I felt I was doing God's will, but in actuality, I had formulated my *own* plans for my life. I had been baptized in the water and the Spirit, but had no spiritual understanding of what God had ordained as my divine purpose.

When my "weights" would weigh me down, I began to find comfort in snacking on food. It became the "weight" that stabilized me back into my comfort zone. While I watched television and sports, I would excessively consume foods to my stomach's content. "The wicked, through the pride of his countenance, will not seek after God: God is not in all his thoughts," (Psalms 10:4). God was not at all in my thoughts, while I conceded to my fleshly desires.

A couple of years of this unhealthy habit resulted in me being overweight. I gained almost seventy pounds over my healthy weight, as I subtly became a captive to my own fleshly habits. I was digging an early grave for myself, while blinded to the reckless lifestyle I was living. No, I was not smoking, drinking, cussing or doing any outward expression of sin that was once evident *before* I received the Holy Spirit, but I was now in a much *worse* state. I was wasting the liberty that I was given, just for the lusts of comfort that the snacking gave me. The "holy" and "perfect" born-again believer was now covered in "weights" that held him captive from fulfilling or even receiving his divine purpose. I was in the "race," but I was handicapped by the "weights" that so quickly became a burden to me.

> "For if any be a hearer of the word, and not a doer, he is like unto a man beholding his natural face in a glass: For he beholdeth himself, and goeth his way, and straightway forgetteth what manner of man he was. But whoso looketh into the perfect law of liberty, and continueth therein, he being not a forgetful hearer, but a doer of the work, this man shall be blessed in his deed," (James 1:23-25).

One day, I looked in the mirror. I could no longer see myself; just a mask that was horrifying to look at. I hated what I saw and became determined to do something about it. I was going to get back into the shape I wanted to be, and I was confident in *myself* to get there. A couple of months passed by, and nothing drastic happened. When I would lose five pounds, I would gain them right back. The harder I tried the fewer results I received.

Finally, I turned to God, and at that moment I became aware of the state I was *truly* in. The more I began to seek and inquire of the Lord, the more He

Break Free

revealed to me the fleshly habits that needed to be eradicated from me. Every time I looked for comfort and picked up something to eat, God would speak to me and softly say, "Don't eat that," or "Stop!" I became totally aware of my poor actions, because now *God* was in my thoughts.

Within the next 12 months, I lost all the weight that I had gained and even *more*. It was not exercising that did it and it was not restricting myself from any foods; it was simply being emptied of my bad habits as well as hearing and obeying the Word of God. Only *then* did I receive the results that I so desperately tried to achieve on my own. There was no workout plan, neither was there a diet; I just stopped trying to carry the load on my own.

At first, I was looking for a quick fix out of my situation. However, when I surrendered to God, He took me through a process that was painful at times, but in the end I reaped the abundant benefits of being obedient. The process did not cause my body weight to disappear when I *immediately* surrendered to God, but it allowed me to follow the path in my "race" that He specifically laid out. That path withdrew me from the laws and limitations that our natural bodies are subject to. God's way completely defied the world's way of losing weight.

Running the Race

~ *The Race of Patience* ~

"... let us run with patience the race that is set before us," (Hebrews 12:1). The "race" we run is to transform us and equip us with the knowledge of our purpose and God's presence. Just as the many clouds of witnesses show the benefits in following the directions of God, we must also lay down our mess and live in the message from our everlasting Father. Abram followed the voice of God out of his homeland to become the father of many nations. Joseph, the dreamer, had to endure many trials and obstacles in seeing the fulfillment of his dreams. David was anointed king of Israel as a young boy, but endured persecution, trials, and tribulations in his journey to the throne.

Could you imagine waiting twenty-five years to see the fulfillment of your promised son, like Abraham? Would you endure thirteen years of afflictions before becoming the deliverer of a nation? What about being anointed for the highest level of authority in your nation as a child, but not receiving it until you were thirty years old?

One of the hardest lessons to learn is being patient, because God's Word is unchanged and unaffected by our situations. We see a need for something to change, but it is not until the Word moves, that we see our situation change. "My brethren, count it all joy when ye fall into divers temptations; Knowing this, that the trying of your faith worketh patience. But let patience have her perfect work, that ye may be perfect and entire, wanting nothing." (James 1:2-4)

Patience is produced in the midst of storms; it blossoms under the intense pressures of the storms. "And not only so, but we glory in tribulations also: knowing that tribulation worketh patience; and patience, experience; and experience, hope:" (Romans 5:3-4). The enemy's goal is to keep us from being patient. Patience is what produces the expectance that the storm will end and the assurance that if we just hold onto the Word, we will receive the rainbow (our promise) at the other end of the storm. So, the enemy uses our natural senses against us to make us lose our patience.

We *hear* carnal advice, we *see* our vulnerability, we *smell* the aroma of convenience and comfort, we *taste* the bitterness of every unwarranted persecution, and we *feel* the pain and the agony of the hail that falls upon us. We are tempted in all points to get out of our situation, and it seems like we are the only ones in the storm. However, just like Abraham, Joseph, David, Jesus Christ and the apostles, we have to endure the temptation to "give up" if we are to ever receive what God has spoken over our lives.

Running the Race

~ Rebelling Against Patience ~

When we become fretful and impatient in our situations, it leads us to rebel against the plan of God. We abort so many blessings when we anxiously make a decision that is contrary to the Word that God instructed us to be obedient to. The seeds of God that are planted inside of us must *stay* in us, so that when the storm comes, they can grow into the manifestation of the fruit of God. What the enemy does *not* tell us, is that the storm is going to come *anyways*, but it is only purposeful to those that have seeds planted in them.

We have to wait on God when our natural senses are tempted. We have to trust His plan when the "race" seems never ending. When we hit the wall of uncertainty, we have to press our way through, even though it may seem hopeless and impossible. For at the "finish line" awaits a reward to those that complete their course holding their position.

~ The Power of Patience ~

The way that we handle our storms determines our outcome when the storm has passed. When we resist the urge to concede to the wall pressing against us, it allows us to realize the power that is in us. Being patient in the midst of extreme pressure produces a greater knowledge of the overcoming strength that has

Break Free

been given to us through the Holy Spirit. In our storm, we are constantly reminded of the importance of waiting on God. We know that in this "race" there is, and will always be, an obstacle trying to block us from our "finish lines."

There are also many distractions to our left and to our right; however, the obstacle is only there for the glory of God to be manifested in our lives. It can be baffling to be doing the will of God and get to a place where we seem cornered. We can not turn back, and the obstacle in front of us is impossible to overcome. We've been anointed the whole time during our journey, but now that we have reached this great wall, we can not feel God anymore. The question, "Where is your God *now*?" arises from onlookers. They have seen us prosper up to this point, and they even were cheering us on, but now that we are faced with this "wall," they see no hope for us. Doubting the calling on our lives and the testimonies we have obtained, they now only see the mountain of a "wall" that no one on earth can defeat. Therefore, we become alone in our lane *and* in our faith.

It is so amazing how the closer we get to our destination in God, the bigger the obstacle becomes. You see a "mountain" from afar off; you know it is big, but the closer you get to the "mountain," the more you realize the true magnitude of its size. It is easy to *start* a race, for the distance does not do justice to the

Running the Race

discipline required to *finish* the race. When we all receive our call, we accept the work with our whole heart. As we commence through the process and chaos breaks loose, only those that are disciplined in the "race" will be able to withstand the pressures of not quitting the "race."

Our "muscles" tense and our bodies fight against the wind. We are compelled forward and we have to keep our form while surrounded by chaotic forces. The more we stay committed to the form, the more we are pushed by an undeniable force. When we stay surrendered to God, in regards to the trials and confusion that exists in our reality, the spirit of God will push us to our destiny through the strength of His Word. We are no longer running under *our* power, but under the influence of the almighty Word of God - Jesus Christ. Our faith in God keeps us focused on the "finish line" and blinds us from our distractions. Where God guides, He will sustain. So, we must walk out the plan of God according to His footsteps, for it is the only way to Him.

~ *The Author and Finisher of Our Faith* ~

"Looking unto Jesus the author and finisher of our faith; who for the joy that was set before him endured the cross, despising the shame, and is set down at the right hand of the throne of God," (Hebrews 12:2).

Break Free

This is the story of Jesus. He performed many miracles. Many believed Him and received their healing and deliverance. Some saw Him get baptized in the Jordan river and heard the voice of God proclaim Him to be the Son of God. He gained disciples that hung on His every word and believed His deity through his authority and miracles. He empowered many through His teachings and gave hope to many. However, when He got closer to His divine destiny, something *changed*.

People began to see the *man*, not the *God* they had been worshipping. He was betrayed by one of his close followers. He was accused of crimes He did not commit. All of His followers left Him as He drew near to the cross. He was beaten, scourged, spit on, reviled, and disfigured just for the pleasure of the same people who had once loved Him. The same multitude that once flocked to Him while the healings and miracles occurred, were the same ones that demanded His death. All alone on earth, He took the shame of *His* "wall" (the cross), *just* for us.

Although undeserving of such love and kindness, He was disfigured beyond recognition, so that we could see the beauty of Love. He was beaten and wounded, so that we could receive eternal healing. He was nailed to the cross, so that we could be freed from the bondage of sin. He died, so that we would never have to bear

Running the Race

our "wall" of death. He rose again, so that we could live a new life reconciled to our Creator without the guilt of our former life. His sacrifice has freed us, and through the guiltless blood of the Lamb, we can overcome every obstacle that comes our way to block us from reaching our destiny.

We don't need to carry "weights," we just have to cover our "walls" with the blood of Jesus and we will be free to enter into rest and cross our "finish line." Every "race" we journey through has a different "destination," a new level in God. Nevertheless, if we are covered by the blood of Jesus and filled with the Word of His testimony for our lives, the same method of winning is ours if we are surrendered to Him. We will then receive our reward at the "finish line."

≈ Birthing a Son ≈

"And let us not be weary in well doing: for in due season we shall reap, if we faint not," (Galatians 6:9).

The Word of God tells us that Jacob loved Rachel, and that in order for him to have her as his wife, he had to agree to work for her father, Laban, for seven years (Genesis 29:18-20). After laboring for seven years, Laban gave Leah to be Jacob's wife instead of Rachel. Laban's reasoning was that he had to give his first-born daughter away in marriage *before* he could give away the *younger* daughter. So, to have Rachel as his wife, Jacob had to commit himself to *another* seven years of labor. Naturally, Laban was taking advantage of Jacob, but Jacob's heart was passionate for Rachel.

After exchanging their vows for each other, Jacob wanted nothing more than to please Rachel. He wanted to make her happy above *anyone* else. Although Jacob "knew" and had children with Leah,

Birthing a Son

Leah's maidservant, Rachel's maidservant, and *not* Rachel, his *heart* was only focused on Rachel. However, the one thing that Jacob could not please Rachel with was baring children, for she was barren. All of his accomplishments were of no value to him if Rachel was not pleased. Unfortunately, Jacob could do nothing in his own power to change Rachel's inability to have a child. It was not until *God* heard the cry of Rachel that her womb was freed and could conceive a baby. "And God remembered Rachel, and God hearkened to her, and opened her womb," (Genesis 30:22).

We *shall* reap, if we faint not. Whatever the actual length of time it takes to receive our "harvest," it is as a few days in comparison to the treasures that we obtain. When we have put in the work to be with *our* "Rachel", our lives are filled with joy because we receive access to enter into intimacy with the One we love. Our "Rachel" is, it brings out the best in us. It forces us to concentrate on fulfilling our divine assignments so that we can ultimately enjoy more intimate time with *our* spouse.

God has called us and continues to equip us throughout the "race." He has defeated giants, removed obstacles, and torn down walls that have been in our way. Now that we have endured the journey, we are ready to gain access to freely dwelling in the presence

Break Free

of God. We can finally receive the things that we have longed for, and no good thing will be withheld from us, for *now* we will appreciate it. "For the LORD God is a sun and shield: the LORD will give grace and glory: no good thing will he withhold from them that walk uprightly," (Psalms 84:11).

~ *The Offspring of Grace* ~

"And it came to pass, when Rachel had born Joseph, that Jacob said unto Laban, Send me away, that I may go unto mine own place, and to my country," (Genesis 30:25).

In our lives we experience the manifestation of the Spirit of God, and similar to Jacob, we too fall in love. So, we fulfill our assignments and obligations just so we can please the Holy Spirit. "Fruit" has been produced from the assignments we have completed, and God's abundance has filled the great voids in our lives.

Nevertheless, the Spirit of God in us remains *barren* of an "offspring." We have experienced the joy of bringing new life into the world through our obedience to the law, but it does not fill our desire to conceive with the One we truly love. Only through the grace of God does the Spirit in us connect to His Word, and open the "womb" of our hearts. Our communion with Him can then "birth" a child of promise into the world. Anyone can write hundreds of books under the

Birthing a Son

instruction of God's Holy Word, but it is a completely different manifestation when the Spirit of God connects to God's Word and conceives in us a "child" born through *love*, and not *obligation*.

~ Stepping out of the Boat ~

Many of us feel obligated to go to church, start ministries, tithe, pray, fast, and use our gifts and talents, for it is the "Christian" thing to do. We receive rewards, gifts, accolades and a good reputation for our obedience, but the child of *promise* is different. Children of promise are not moved out of fear of regulation or obligation, but rather radically led by an inner drive to go out into deeper and uncharted territory. It is beyond the rationalization of theology and doctrine. It dwells void of legalism and regulations. It is rooted in the never ending heart of God.

"And Peter answered him and said, Lord, if it be thou, bid me come unto thee on the water. And he said, Come. And when Peter was come down out of the ship, he walked on the water, to go to Jesus," (Matthew 14:28-29).

There was a desire in Peter that wanted to experience something impossible, but he could not accomplish it off of his *own* words; he needed *Jesus* to bid him to come. With *one* word, Peter experienced something that no other man, besides Jesus, has ever

Break Free

experienced. He walked into uncharted territory. No other disciple made the request or even dared to step out of the boat. They did not even know if it was *Jesus*; they were committed to staying in the boat after Jesus had instructed them to get on the boat (Matthew 14:22). So, *alone*, Peter walked on the Word to "come" to Jesus in the midst of a violent sea.

How tragic it is that we *overly* highlight the fact that Peter took his eyes off of Jesus as he regarded the sea and began to drown. *We* would have done the same thing. But through the grace of God, as we reach *our* "wall" of fear, God pulls us out of certain destruction and allows us to dwell safely in His presence. All the disciples on the boat glorified Jesus for such a miracle, but it was only Peter that had enough courage to step out of obligation and past instructions. Through the grace of God, a miracle was birthed in the midst of overwhelming circumstances.

It was not *Peter* that performed the miracle, but it was the Word that went forth out of Jesus' mouth that could not come back to Him void. (Isaiah 55:11) Will *we* step out of the boat and allow God to do the impossible in *our* lives? Will we act on the invitation to come? Or will we stay on the boat waiting for Jesus to come to *us*? It is entirely up to us.

≈ Sown Seeds of Promise ≈

"Through wisdom is an house builded; and by understanding it is established:" (Proverbs 24:3).

We can love God and be focused on pleasing Him, but we need an understanding of His Word to experience true intimacy with Him. God is not moved by our feelings or our emotions, but by our faith through the understanding of His Word. Many of us receive the baptism of the Holy Spirit, but never see the manifestation of its power. We are busy trying to please the Spirit our *own* way instead of surrendering ourselves to the word of God and allowing Him to perform miracles through us.

In our society, we will not take a job unless the pay *and* benefits meet or exceed what we desire. No one wants to work and not receive a paycheck at the end of the pay period. I once had a job that laid me off for two weeks, and then called me in to work a forty hour week. When I received my paycheck, I was looking forward to the large amount of money that my family needed to pay bills. When I opened my check, I saw that it had been written for *two* dollars, and the rest went towards paying my family's health insurance company. I decided that from that day forward, no matter what amount I received on my paycheck, I was not going to be dependent on my *job* to pay my bills and feed my family; I had to completely trust in *God* to supply our needs.

Question, do you tithe on *two* dollars? We have to understand that it is not about the amount of money, it is about our obedience to God's Word. Our tithe is not a seed that we decide to sow, it is *already* God's. Many of us tithe so we can receive a financial reward from God, but He is more than an avenue to obtain monetary wealth. Our tithes may lead us to our reward, for it is a step of obedience. What happens, though, with the remaining ninety percent that we have? How do we effectively sow seeds to produce a plenteous harvest in our lives?

It is simple, forsake everything in our lives and follow God with all that we have. It is easy to inspire and motivate *other* people to change, using our gifts and talents, but when *we* are faced with the question of forsaking our money, our luxuries, our conveniences, and our securities, *we* place a "wall" up. We become envious of others' financial prosperity and criticize

Break Free

them, for we are looking at them with jealousy. We strangle the Word of God in our lives in an effort to maintain our conveniences. However we do not realize that we are limiting *our* "harvest," because there are no seed being sown.

I used to be very judgmental of others, when I did not understand their success. I would look for the smallest "spot" on them to justify myself in being "glad" that I was not like them. The fact of the matter, however, is that someone walking in the "harvest" of the Lord could not care less of what others think about them because they are simply reaping the "harvest" of what God told them to sow.

Fortunately, when I finally examined myself according to the Word of God, I was freed from the spirit of judging others. Through my examination, God also freed me from many other evil spirits that were dwelling in me. Through His love, He would convict me and I would give up anything that I held in a higher regard than Him. When I gave things away, I had to turn and not look back. When I sold my things, I always received less than what I had originally paid for my possessions.

My sports cards were *priceless* to me for sentimental reasons. I had collected them since I was a child and I never imagined that I would be giving them away nor selling them, period. Through a painful exchange, I surrendered the cards so that I could be released to go into a deeper relationship with the Lord. Although they were worth way more than five thousand dollars, I only received one hundred and twenty dollars for them. It was a humbling experience for me to be so attached to so many things that I had valued for years, and have them gone instantly, for almost *nothing*.

~ Revelation of Seeds ~

For years, I was obedient in letting go of things, with no understanding exactly of what I was receiving in return. I would ignorantly take the money I received and waste it. Then, God spoke to me and said, "When you sell your possessions, you are not just receiving *money*, you are receiving a *seed*." That revelation changed my life. Instead of looking for my possessions to give me a *reward*, I received "seeds" that were necessary to sow, so a "harvest" could be produced in my life. All that time I was receiving "seeds" that were there to change my life, but I devalued instead, because I thought that just getting those things out of my possession was enough. However, without a "seed" sown, how will we reap a "harvest?"

God revealed that when we forsake our idols, possessions, worldly things, and our lives, we are empty so that when we receive a "seed," it can be planted in cultivated ground. In the process of time, that "seed" will grow, and we will reap a "harvest." The unplanted "seed" was never intended to sustain us. Whatever we receive is a "seed" that has to be sown into a person or something that God has placed in our hearts.

~ *Yet Thou Lackest One Thing* ~

"And a certain ruler asked him, saying, Good Master, what shall I do to inherit eternal life? And Jesus said unto him, Why callest thou me good? none is good, save one, that is, God. Thou knowest the commandments, Do not commit adultery, Do not kill, Do not steal, Do not bear false witness, Honour thy father and thy mother. And he said, All these have I kept from my youth up. Now when Jesus heard these things, he said unto him, Yet lackest thou one thing: sell all that thou hast, and distribute unto the poor, and thou shalt have treasure in heaven: and come, follow me. And when he heard this, he was very sorrowful: for he was very rich," (Luke 18:18-23).

There is a young and rich ruler in all of us. Yes, we possess many great qualities, but there is "one thing" that is void in our hearts, and *that* is what God is looking to fill.

"Then Jesus beholding him loved him, and said unto him, One thing thou lackest: go thy way, sell whatsoever thou hast, and give to the poor, and thou shalt have treasure in heaven: and come, take up the cross, and follow me," (Mark 10:21).

Why did Jesus ask the ruler to sell all his possessions, give up his power and go follow Him? That *hurts*, how is that *love*? That command is one that challenges our fears and isolates us from Him. None of us want to give up the things we treasure, because it will leave us in a vulnerable state. So, many of us walk *away* from God's command and live without fulfilling His Will by following Jesus.

We have to be emptied of ourselves so we can follow God wherever He wants to take us. Will we allow our possessions keep us from the reward that God has for us? If we let them, our possessions can keep us from seeing the *unlimited* treasure that God has for us. Like the ruler, we want to be justified in the presence of the "Good Master," but when he chastens us, we walk away from following Him because what it is that He is asking from us, we are not willing to give up.

We want the reward of Heaven through our conditional devotion in fulfilling the law. Through our religion and traditions we have settled our hearts in obtaining heaven through our many works. "Christ is become of no effect unto you, whosoever of you are justified by the law; ye are fallen from grace," (Galatians 5:4). We feel qualified through our many

Break Free

efforts of kindness and dedication, but that "one thing" remains missing in our lives. If we knew what God *really* thought about us, would we be willing to change if we knew we were in the wrong? Does God find pleasure in rituals or obligation? We can follow principles and guidelines, but they can only get us so far. They may lead us towards God, but in order to dwell in His presence, there has to be a sacrifice. This was the missing element of the ruler as well as what is missing in all of us.

We have ruled our lives when we have fed the poor, helped the lowly and downtrodden, comforted the sorrowful and encouraged the lost. We have always controlled how and when to do good works for others, but then Jesus suddenly asks us to hand over everything that we have possessed and ruled. That seems like too much to give up, but it is only those of us that sacrifice our lives that will be able to follow God to the depths that He wants to take us to.

"Then Peter said, Lo, we have left all, and followed thee. And he said unto them, Verily I say unto you, There is no man that hath left house, or parents, or brethren, or wife, or children, for the kingdom of God's sake, Who shall not receive manifold more in this present time, and in the world to come life everlasting," (Luke 18:28-30).

Sown Seeds of Promise

When we forsake everything, our hearts are no longer pulled by things or people, but rather by the Spirit of God. We become completely dependent on God, *period*. Our hearts are emptied of the pollution of this world, and we are able to be filled with the love of God. This does not mean that we will live a life of a beggar; it simply means that we are solely dependent on God to provide for us so we can do more for Him. It is not *what* we receive, nor the *abundance* of things that distinguishes if we are blessed, but it is the freedom that we gain to be able to follow God with no restraints.

≈ *What is our Reward?* ≈

"What is my reward then? Verily that, when I preach the gospel, I may make the gospel of Christ without charge, that I abuse not my power in the gospel. For though I be free from all men, yet have I made myself servant unto all, that I might gain the more. And unto the Jews I became as a Jew, that I might gain the Jews; to them that are under the law, as under the law, that I might gain them that are under the law; To them that are without law, as without law, (being not without law to God, but under the law to Christ,) that I might gain them that are without law. To the weak became I as weak, that I might gain the weak: I am made all things to all men, that I might by all means save some," (I Corinthians 9:18-22).

If our reward is not in what we receive, what *is* our reward? Where *do* we find contentment and satisfaction? When we commit to God and forsake our lives to follow Jesus, our hearts must be rested and secure in our relationship with Him. In our state of emptiness we are dependent on God to provide all of our needs, but it is a lot easier *said*, than *done*. The

What is Our Reward

apostles suffered outrageous persecution for their relationship with Jesus Christ. Many became martyrs for the cause of spreading the gospel to the lost. Many were vessels that God used who endured obstacles and afflictions to empower others through the Holy Word.

In the midst of their circumstances, God used people to demonstrate His power and love so that *we* could come to know Him for ourselves. So, what makes *us* so special to be exempted from trials and sufferings today? We want the abundance of God's rewards, but when suffering comes along will we choose to lean on *them* instead of depending on *God*?

The reward that we have longed for is simply found in the aroma of a sweet smelling sacrifice.

"Greater love hath no man than this, that a man lay down his life for his friends. Ye are my friends, if ye do whatsoever I command you. Henceforth I call you not servants; for the servant knoweth not what his lord doeth: but I have called you friends; for all things that I have heard of my Father I have made known unto you. Ye have not chosen me, but I have chosen you, and ordained you, that ye should go and bring forth fruit, and that your fruit should remain: that whatsoever ye shall ask of the Father in my name, he may give it you. These things I command you, that ye love one another," (John 15:13-17).

Break Free

There is no greater act than to lay down our lives for our friends. To suffer naturally, so that others can be healed *spiritually*, is the true treasure of a follower of Christ. We that believe in God endure many storms. However, the storms are there for us to learn to lean on God's strength.

We can then obtain a testimony that will strengthen our brethren that are still in captivity. Although the apostle Paul was put in prison, he did not dwell in self pity, but his eyes were focused on his brethren. In spite of his state of captivity, God uses Paul's epistles to liberate the lives of many readers to this day. In the heart of the wilderness, David gave his heart to God, and by his writings in the book of Psalms, has encouraged many to continue with Lord.

When we follow Jesus, our lives are secure in salvation, and we take on captivity to liberate the lost. So, our reward is not what we obtain, but in the liberation of the captives of this world. When we share our gifts with others, our experiences, and battles it allows them to see the light of God that they have been blinded from; opening their hearts to the love of God. Despite our good or bad situations, our reward is to see others reconciled back into communion with God. As we dwell in the presence of God, our treasure is our relationship with Him.

What is Our Reward

"For God, who commanded the light to shine out of darkness, hath **shined in our hearts**, to **give the light** of the knowledge of the glory of God in the face of Jesus Christ. But we have this treasure in earthen vessels, **that the excellency of the power may be of God, and not of us**. We are troubled on every side, yet not distressed; we are perplexed, but not in despair; Persecuted, but not forsaken; cast down, but not destroyed; Always bearing about in the body the dying of the Lord Jesus, that the life also of Jesus might be made manifest in our body. For we which live are always delivered unto death for Jesus' sake, that the life also of Jesus might be made manifest in our mortal flesh. **So then death worketh in us, but life in you**. We having the same spirit of faith, according as it is written, I believed, and therefore have I spoken; we also believe, and therefore speak; Knowing that he which raised up the Lord Jesus shall raise up us also by Jesus, and shall present us with you. **For all things are for your sakes**, that the abundant grace might through the thanksgiving of many redound to the glory of God. For which cause we faint not; but though our outward man perish, yet the inward man is renewed day by day. For **our light affliction**, which is but for a moment, **worketh for us a far more exceeding and eternal weight of glory**; While we look not at the things which are seen, but at the things which are not seen: **for the things which are seen are temporal; but the things which are not seen are eternal**," (II Corinthians 4:3-18).

Hallelujah!! This is our purpose, to live free in Christ so that others can walk in the same freedom of serving our great and loving God. *Break Free* and live

Break Free

in the joy of reconciling a world back into relationship with our Lord and Savior Jesus Christ.

About the Author

E'yen has a strong passion to spread the gospel of Jesus Christ to everyone. His passion is extended through many areas, one of which he is the chief writer for, *Step Into Fold*, a blog that bares his transparency and love for God's people (view at: www.stepintofold.blogspot.com). E'yen co-teaches the Young Adult Class for the Sunday School Department, and is a Youth Leader for Teens at his church home.

E'yen is a supportive husband to his wife and "crown" of 9 years, Maia Gardner, and is an active and devoted father to his six children (Arin, J'sun, Raya, Lesa, Kyan and Bria).

E'yen loves to write, dance, and teach. Some of his hobbies include playing sports, running, spending time with his wife and children, reading and watching movies.

To order books, leave testimonies, have prayer requests or to donate to our company, contact us at:

Printed Word Publishing
P.O. Box 360812
Columbus, Ohio 43236

WEBSITE: www.pwpublish.com
EMAIL: pwpublish@yahoo.com
PHONE: 614-678-5353
FAX: 1-888-221-3166

Thank you for your prayers and support.

LaVergne, TN USA
13 November 2009
164116LV00001B/1/P